Seasons

A Real Story of an Amish Girl

❖　　❖　　❖

Elizabeth Byler Younts

SEASONS
Published by EBY Books

Scripture quotations or paraphrases are taken from the King
James Version.

The characters of this book are based solely on the memories of
Lydia Lee Coblentz. With the exception of family members,
names have been changed.

Cover Design: Christopher Dack
Front Cover Photography: Esther Coblentz Byler
Front Cover Model: Celine Esther Jeanne Mutzke
Back Cover Photography: Elizabeth Byler Younts
Back Cover Model: Lydia Lee Coblentz

Published in the United States of America.

Byler Younts, Elizabeth
    Seasons/Elizabeth Byler Younts, — 1st ed
    ISBN: 978-1461148678

Printed in the United States of America
2011

Seasons

Dedication

For

Mammie, your stories blossomed in my summer,

*Mom and Dad, your encouragement in my spring has been a
double rainbow that never fades,*

and

for Davis, my every season is yours. I love you eternally.

Preface

Dear Reader,

In one of my earliest memories, I am four years old and visiting my grandparents. I was wearing yellow pajamas that I thought were fancy and I took residence on one of my *mammie's* knees–my grandma, Lydia Lee Coblentz. One of my many cousins sat on the other. Mammie read us a story. While I don't remember anything about the story, I remember her lap was warm and comfortable and that she had thick hands, undoubtedly from years and years of hard work. The scent of baked bread and dish soap always seemed to linger around her.

As a child, I could never have understood how those hands had labored and how her heart had grieved. As a girl not much older than I was in those easy days of my childhood, she was already carrying heavy burdens. More than twenty-five years later, as this book began to take shape, I was moved with how God so gently carried her heart through the most desperate of times. It gave me an even greater respect for her.

While I took some liberties on verbal and internal dialog, I wrote *Seasons* as closely based on Mammie's memories as possible. Many, but not all, names have been changed upon her request. When reading a shared memory or one you have often heard through the years, be gracious, as everyone remembers and interprets things differently. I want this book to honor the amazing life that God has given this wonderful woman in my life.

I am so thankful for my heritage and feel privileged that I was trusted with writing these memories. I pray you enjoy this book and that you share it with friends.

Blessings,
Elizabeth

Acknowledgements

I want to thank my grandma, *Mammie*. Thank you for your patience. How I loved our conversations about your life.

Mom, thank you for never giving up on me. For always encouraging me to write this story. It was a labor of love for us both and without your help, persistence, and unfailing belief in me, it could never have happened.

I want to say thank you to my husband, Davis. You are such a rock. You have this amazing ability to let me bloom at my own pace. You are unlike any person I know.

Felicity and Mercy, my dearest little women, I say thank you because having a mother for a writer (I mean a writer for a mother) can be a lot for little ones.

Thank you to my dear niece, Celine. You were the perfect *Liddy* stand in.

Thank you to my cousin, Irene, for documenting and gathering so many valuable stories. I can't tell you how much those handwritten notes helped me.

I must thank Christopher Dack, for all the technical typography work and my beautiful cover—you have been such an integral part of making this book come to life. I'm indebted to you!

To my pre-publication readers: Christy, Becky, Chris, Mike, Shana, Sena, Anna, Victoria, Chantelle, Monica, and Adrienne; each of you improved the readability of this book. Thank you for your honesty and encouragement.

A huge shout out to my weekly critique group—Allison P., Raquel, Roxanne, Allison J., Ken, Monica, Irma, and Debbie. I am so grateful for each of you. Not a Monday night will go by where I won't wish myself gathered around the table with you all—even though the Air Force had the gall to move me far, far away.

And, thank you to Allison Pittman, so much more than a critique partner and writing mentor. I cannot put into words how grateful I am for you. To count you among my closest friends is a blessing from our Heavenly Father. I consider you my sister.

And, above all, to my Savior, Jesus Christ, the Author of all stories, words, and life; to You I give all the praise.

Winter

Prologue

Living in Vermontville, Michigan (2011)

An Old Lady Speaks

I ONCE HAD a friend who bent down to tie her shoe and never made it back up. She died. She had just turned eighty.

I celebrated my own eightieth birthday surrounded by my entire family and many friends. Despite missing my dear husband and my son, who both passed through their winter seasons all too early, I had a wonderful day. I got out of bed, tied my shoes, and enjoyed the big surprise party waiting for me at my son David's house.

Every birthday naturally ushers in great eagerness for what's next, but worry is guaranteed to follow for the same reason. Aging has its benefits; I know that days turn to years overnight. I know that the ebb and flow of life can unfortunately become more captivating than celebrating the season God wants us to live out.

The Bible talks about these seasons of life. It says, *To every thing there is a season, and a time to every purpose under the heaven: A time to be born, and a time to die; ... A time to weep, and a time to laugh; a time to mourn, and a time to dance; ... A time to love, and a time to hate; a time of war, and a time of peace.*

Each season is filled with storms of death and loss that, nonetheless, provide comfort in their fulfillment. I've experienced great happiness and sadness, as everyone does. When I reminisce on my early years and how God used them to shape and prepare me, I am in awe.

When considering my life I am struck by my season of spring. It's a journey of love lost and found, heartbreak, fears, and even dreams come true. I am not sure that in my later seasons I would feel so deeply, love so strongly, and strive with such desperation if it weren't for what I experienced as a young girl in the bittersweet spring of my life.

Here are my memories, how I remember the season of my girlhood.

Welcome to spring.

Spring

One

Living on Hazelville Road (1926–1933)

A Little Girl Content

"LIDDY! LIDDY!" *MEMM* called. "*Ich muss dei hilve.*" My mom called for my help.

Even in a stiff autumn wind her high, sweet voice could find my ears. I was convinced it could find me anywhere. And that if I were lost, it would lovingly guide me home. A dim glow surrounded my mom's form, creating a silhouette in the doorway of my little farmhouse.

"I'm almost finished," I called to her. She waved back and returned inside.

As I moved faster the wind picked up, and the lantern hanging in the window creaked against the rusty nail. I knew the lantern wasn't safe there on a windy night, but that nail was the only one I could reach. Now it swung like a pendulum, back and forth, back and forth, and the eerie noise made me work faster. I made sure the horse was fed and that Dat wouldn't have much to do once he came in from the orchard.

A chill caught me and I dropped the pitchfork to retie my headscarf. Loose threads from the frayed, royal blue fabric came away between my fingers. It was so thin and worn, my ears were frozen despite its covering. I needed to mention it to Memm. It was October and my seventh birthday was around the corner. It couldn't be too much to ask for a new headscarf as a gift.

I unhooked the lantern and hurried out of the barn. The cold temperature seized my body. I hugged my too-small, navy blue coat tightly with one hand, and lantern with the other, making sure the round glow encompassed me. My feet stepped hard and fast across the frozen ground. Though I had no real reason to be frightened, I always ran from the barn to our small two-story farmhouse. In the small circle of light, everything behind me looked ghostly, and everything ahead was always too many steps away.

I hit the porch steps like a horse against the newly paved roads in the countryside outside of Dover. My toes stung. I wished we had more money so I could buy thick store-bought socks and new shoes like my schoolmates wore. The Bishop of our Amish church said that the Ten Commandments spoke against coveting someone else's belongings, but I wasn't trying to sin; I just wanted to be warm.

Once I made it through the front door, I headed straight for the wood stove without shedding my coat. I rubbed my hands in the steam of the potato soup that simmered for supper. I peeked in the smaller pot and the scent of the onion found my nose in an instant. A few bits of onions and boiled beats were always a treat. In all honesty, though, my taste buds craved the flavor of venison or beef. I pushed those thoughts away, knowing discontentment was a sin. My stomach growled, and though it didn't seem fair, I asked God to forgive me for wishing it were full of food.

As I warmed myself, my five-year-old sister, Tillie, swept at a snail's pace. Her imagination took her far away, making every movement slower than the previous one. As the eldest of five in the Lee home, I couldn't do anything slowly. I wore my responsibility like a piece of clothing Memm dutifully made. I admit, there were times I was jealous of Tillie's easy-going ways, but being the eldest held a standard of duty that I longed for, that I was born for. It was one of the few things a daughter in a poor family could claim as her very own. Still, I had to be careful not to feel prideful in my ability to quickly accomplish every task my parents gave me.

"Liddy," Memm said, turning toward me as she dried a pot that reflected like a mirror. I could see the signs of her hard work on her apron at the peak of her belly while the rest of her white apron remained clean.

"Finish sweeping then set the table. Tillie, round up the little ones. *Dat* will be home soon."

Tillie and I did as we were told, and my dad walked into the house less than ten minutes later. Memm always knew when he would be home, without fail.

Dat's entrance into the house was quiet, which was typical. He wasn't one to make a stir. He gave Memm a little nod, and when her face lit with an ever-so-slight smile, the deep lines on his wind-burned forehead softened in response. I loved his weathered skin and decided that I would never marry a man with a smooth face and hands, for that would be a clear sign he wasn't a hard worker.

While Dat washed up for supper, I busied myself setting the table with mixed and matched dinner plates for Memm, Dat and me, and enamel bowls for the rest. None of our silverware matched, which didn't bother me. The worn and dented tin cans we used for cups, however, were like a constant ache, reminding me that we were poor. I wasn't ashamed; I was sad. Even after doing our best to keep the sharp edges filed down, we suffered several cut lips. This week Tillie got a new can that nearly sparkled, but it was still a tin can.

I'd overheard my schoolteacher, Mrs. Mable Massey, talking with another teacher about ordering new drinking glasses from the Sears and Roebuck's catalog. I imagined, just for a moment, drinking iced tea on a hot summer day. But when I lifted the imaginary glass to my lips, the rough ripple of the tin can brought me back to reality. Truly, it was wrong not to be thankful, so I just did my best to keep our tin cans as clean and polished as I could.

I pulled the benches out on either side of the small, rickety table and filled Dat's can with weak coffee. A visiting family had given us a jar of Postum a few months ago. I remember watching my mom peel away the seal slowly, inhaling deeply and smiling. Though I never asked, I wondered if she'd ever had real coffee without watering it down. She instructed me right away to ration the coffee-flavored drink for Dat only, using half a serving for the morning and half for the evening so the jar would last double the time. She also said to use water, instead of the suggested milk.

I listened carefully and followed her instructions. Then I'd always watch how Dat savored the hot drink even in its weakest form. After supper, while I helped my mom clean up, he would add more scalding water to what was left to make it last through his evening Bible reading while sitting in his hickory rocker.

Dat entered the kitchen just as I finished the table. He smoothed down the thinning black hair that sprung in disarray from wearing his felt farm hat in the cold weather. His hair never lay flat, and I knew my hair would do the same if it wasn't pinned back in a bun beneath my covering. My dark curls were so tight and unruly that I could only brush through them right after a bath.

"Pitch fork wasn't put away, Liddy." His deep voice resonated in my ears as his eyes caught mine.

In a moment I retraced my steps and cringed, remembering where I'd left the dangerous tool.

"Sorry, Dat. I'll make sure to put it where it belongs from now on." I hoped he hadn't tripped over it.

"Had the lantern turned up so I saw it right off." His monotone voice carried authority in every syllable. "You'll be spanked if it happens again."

I nodded, trying to hide a nervous swallow.

Dat walked over to the closed staircase leading to the upstairs where the four younger kids played and called them to dinner, using nothing louder than his speaking voice.

"*Kinnah, zeit fa essa.*"

Rapid footsteps hit the staircase. Tillie, holding baby Edwin, came first followed by Bertha and Albert behind her. They quickly climbed into their respective seats. With another baby on the way, Memm's lap was disappearing, so I took Edwin onto mine and held his hands under the table during the silent prayer. The wall clock ticked loudly in the silence. Twenty-one ticks, always.

I fed Edwin from my plate. Memm patted his cottony dark hair when he reached for her. I was sure he longed to sit on our mom's soft lap instead of my own bony one, but he was soon content with his bottle of watered down milk and a few spoonfuls of thin potato soup.

As the eldest daughter of Dan and Katie Lee, I was learning all about sacrifice as my hungry little brother wanted more than his share of food. I fed him what I had, knowing there would be nothing more for me. I just chewed my piece of bread a little more slowly and drank more water out of my dulled tin can. Then, without a word, Memm spooned the rest of her potatoes onto my plate. I caught her eye for a moment and smiled in thanks. I recorded this sacrifice in my mind so that I could someday be the kind of mother she was to me. Thankfulness swelled my heart, despite such a meager meal. We sat together around the table each night in our safe small house on the orchard.

Two

Living on Hazelville Road (Autumn, 1933)

Rainy Days

THE DAY SMELLED like lemon meringue and tree sap. I breathed it in, wanting the sweetness of it to consume me. When I opened my eyes I saw a flock of birds flying in zigzags against the blue sky. Where were they going? Were they trying to find food? Memm had sent me out an hour ago to pick the late sprouting beans and peppermint tea leaves. There was plenty of peppermint in my regular patch, but I only had a few small handfuls of beans. I reckoned dinner would be skimpy tonight.

Hearing the beans jostle around in the small, tin bucket reminded me of an often told story. When I was just a baby my parents had me checked by a doctor because I'd been crying and whining for days. Sure enough, I'd pushed a navy bean up my nose and it had begun to sprout. I almost blush at the embarrassing act now, but can't help but wish that bean had sprouted in some rich soil nearby. Perhaps we would have more beans tonight for supper if it had.

Times were difficult for us and they were getting worse. Over the past few days my dad had been forced to give away bushels upon bushels of peaches to our neighbors. Memm graciously helped those just as needy as us gather the fruit for their hungry families, though they'd already begun to rot. Dat and Daniel, the Amish preacher who worked for us, had traveled throughout Delaware and even Pennsylvania to sell the crop, but their efforts had been unsuccessful. Giving the peaches away meant something good would come from the fruit rather than callously letting them spoil.

"Thank you, Mr. Lee," an English neighbor woman said. She had a houseful of children to feed. "After breakfast we didn't have any more food in the house. These peaches will feed us for a few more days along with the bread your wife kindly gave us. God bless you."

She gave Memm a hug before leaving. Then, overwhelmed, my mom returned to the house and wept.

"This is all I found," I said to my mom, handing her the small bucket of beans.

The lines on Memm's face deepened but she didn't say a word. Somehow, by the time supper came, Memm had made what little food we had stretch to feed our entire family. Potatoes and beets were mainstays, with the occasional onion to add flavor to our bland meals. We had bread for every meal, and many times it was all we had. It made me think about the story in the Bible about Jesus feeding those crowds of 5,000 people with only a few fish and loaves. I wondered what kind of miracle it would take to feed my family of eight.

I imagined it was hardest on the little ones. Tillie, Bertha and I understood our family's situation, but the boys Albert, Edwin and John didn't. They were hungry, hungrier than I. I had trained my stomach not to expect much, but how can you tell such a young child that the food is gone when they've just begun eating?

Sometimes, during these especially hungry days, I'd imagine being a part of the first Thanksgiving. They feasted for days. How I longed to eat a meal like that. Then I would feel guilty for being discontented and I would consider all the things that I could be thankful for.

I loved my parents, sisters, and brothers.

We were all generally healthy.

I loved school and my teacher Mrs. Massey.

We had a house.

We had peaches to eat and to give away.

Within days of giving away almost our entire harvest of peaches Dat told us that we were leaving the orchard and would have to sell everything we owned. I held my breath as he spoke. I was even more afraid than when my Uncle Amos would tease us about the boogieman behind the barn. The only thing that frightened me more were the hours of Memm's worst labor pains, just before the baby would arrive. I always feared she wouldn't make it through even one more. That was my worst fear.

My mind numbed as I helped my mom scrub down the house. I moved quickly but everything blurred in front of me. Memm cried a lot, her strength waning. When she cried so did my sisters and I.

We labeled every item in our home with a dollar amount, hoping it would sell and we'd somehow have enough money to pay for another rental home. I knew we needed the money, but I secretly hoped our things wouldn't sell because they were a part of my family— part of me. I wanted them to stay with us. How could I see the only things I'd ever known go away to strangers?

I didn't want to say good-bye to the couch where my mom taught me to patch pants. It made my stomach turn to think that someone else would sit in Dat's hickory rocker. I could see in my mind's eye all of us kids around his feet as he read to us from the Bible—about creation, the flood, Daniel and the lion's den, the birth of Jesus, and so much more. Would those stories sound the same from an unfamiliar chair, in a strange home with different furniture—or no furniture at all? Memories flooded my mind: working in the kitchen with Memm, moving around each other like a dance. All of us children had been born here, little John only a short time ago.

I always knew we were poor, but in this season of my young life I struggled not to become bitter about our circumstances. I tried to remember the scripture verse the Preacher spoke about in church on Sunday but my paralyzed mind drew a blank. I closed my eyes, squeezed them shut, trying to keep the tears from escaping. When I opened my eyes I saw our sofa being carried out by two young Amish boys whose dad had just paid a few dollars for it.

My head spun and I felt my stomach flip over on itself. I wanted to go to my room and sit in the corner and cry. Only, it wasn't my room anymore. This wasn't even my home. These thoughts betrayed my heart because I was sure I'd never consider any other house a home.

I remember right where I stood when jolly Uncle Amos recounted holding me for the first time. He told me that he'd been shocked at my curly hair and was glad I'd been born ugly because that meant I would be pretty when I got older. I remember laughing at his words though I didn't understand what he meant until I was much older. Why did things have to change? Uncle Amos and Aunt Molly lived so close now.

Would they be within walking distance at our new house?

I walked to the closed staircase. I could hear every bump-bump from when baby John had fallen down the stairs. Even now my face grew hot with anxiety because it had been my fault. I'd been playing house with the baby and he'd gotten away from me and tumbled all the way down the staircase. For a few moments I was sure I'd killed him, but after some tears from little John and the rest of us in our worry, he was fine. Visions of his happy smile warmed me, though I wondered what would've happened had he been hurt. His safety had been evidence of God's protection. And, now, in these desperate moments, I longed to feel His protecting hand.

I moved past a few well-to-do English women who were looking at the quilts my parents had gotten for their wedding and a few Amish ladies who were comforting Memm, telling her they wished they could help. Our church district helped all they could, but everyone was poor. No one had anything extra to spare.

Needing to spend some time alone, I walked to the small barn. I loved the barn. It was often my only time alone. Sometimes, because I was the oldest, I would help my dad in the barn and we'd work together. We worked well together. He was such a quiet man. He often let me go on and on about my day at school, or we'd sing a hymn. His deep bass voice echoed in the corners of the old barn as I stood there, missing those moments already.

The shed was mostly bare. An old shovel stood lonesome in the corner and a few odds and ends sat on the dusty shelving. The farm tools had been the first to go. The emptiness looked so strange. At least the smell of the old wood and manure and straw was familiar enough. I kicked a few wisps of straw and wished it would make a sound against my shoe. I really wanted to make a racket. Maybe it would help explain how I felt.

God must be here now, I forced myself to believe. But where? The rain began tap-tapping almost like an answer. As my eyes went up, I wished I could see through the dusty ceiling into His heavens.

Tillie rushed into the barn, spinning me back into reality. Tears streaked her face and the hair around her forehead and temples had pulled out from her covering and were in disarray around her face. Her blue eyes were glassy and rain dotted the shoulders of her dress.

"Liddy, Liddy," she said, pulling at my arm. "It's terrible, worse than you can know."

"What?" I asked, a little irritated.

Tillie grabbed me by the shoulders and shook my bean-pole frame. She didn't look six with the worry in her eyes.

"We don't even have a table anymore. Where are we going to eat?"

Where are we going to eat? I thought. I was far more worried about what we were going to eat.

I wasn't angry when I began to cry. I was exhausted from feeling afraid of what was coming next. I walked out of the barn, leaving Tillie to cry alone. The rain came down harder and I could see lightning in the distance and the thunder that followed felt as if it was bursting from within my very soul. My sweet life was suddenly so—so *fahoodled*—a complete mess.

I walked slowly back toward the house, letting the rain drench me to the bone. I stood on the porch and found an ounce of thankfulness when I noticed the activity in the house had slowed. I could see my parents through the window of one of the small bedrooms. Dat was quietly and sweetly comforting Memm. He whispered something in her ear and when she looked up at him she smiled, tears streaked her cheeks.

I lifted my face to the rain and let it wash over me. Then, concerned about the wetness ruining my covering I pulled the pins out quickly and set it under the porch. I returned to the rain, almost believing it was God Himself enveloping me. If my parents could find contentment in this anxious season of our lives, then I could too. I found myself smiling.

My reverie was interrupted by the sound of Memm calling from the window.

"Liddy! *Grick die kapp!*" Get your covering! Just then, a bolt of lightning crossed the sky.

She didn't have to say what I knew she was thinking. Getting hit by lightning was one thing...but getting hit by lightning without my head covering—I didn't want to consider the consequences.

Three

Living at the Hostetler Farm (1933–1934)

In the Bull Pen

IT WAS EARLY in the morning, and I had my face pressed up against the small window near my bed. Snowing again, and not yet Thanksgiving. The room I shared with my sisters was a bit smaller than at the other house, but Memm made it comfortable, and we were given a fair amount of blankets to keep us warm through the already bitterly cold winter.

I used the side of my fist to wipe away the frost that had formed on the inside of the window and licked my hand, refreshing my dry mouth for a moment. I always enjoyed the quietness of the morning. My sisters were still asleep, though I wasn't sure how. I rarely slept past five. An internal clock *tick-tocked* inside my head until I gave in and opened my eyes. My stomach would groan and moan, and I'd wonder if I'd get more than a slice of buttered bread and some watered down milk for breakfast.

My sisters breathed evenly and seemed to rest so soundly. The wooden slats on the floor were freezing, and a draft always seemed to come beneath the crack of the door, so Memm did her best to layer up blankets on the three of us as we slept on a straw tick on the floor. I wasn't sure when we'd get a bed frame again, though I was very thankful that several pieces of furniture were generously returned to us.

My breath was white in front of my face, yet warm enough to create a clear spot to look through to the yard outside. All was gray and black. I heard a door open and shut in the house and saw Dat walk across the drive, moving toward the main part of the farm to begin his daily chores. He walked hunched over and held his hat on his head with one hand. Must be a stiff wind out there. My toes curled up at the thought of it. My shoes had fallen apart a few weeks before, and it would still be another week or so before I would get a new pair. Even though the bottoms of my feet felt like an old piece of leather from going barefoot, I was really looking forward to getting shoes.

Later, when several other pupils, my sisters, and I were sitting in Mrs. Massey's car heading to Rose Valley Elementary School, I sat on top of my feet to warm them. My thankfulness toward my teacher could not be expressed. How much colder would my feet be if I had to walk the several miles each day?

"Just wait for the springtime, girls," Mrs. Massey said in her usual cheerfulness. "We'll put the top down and the warm wind will make us feel like we're flying."

We all giggled and chattered about that the rest of the way.

As we arrived at school I pulled off my coat and black bonnet and hung them on my hook. Next to my patched-up coat hung a beautiful emerald green wool coat with gold buttons. I couldn't stop myself from touching it, imagining for a moment what it would feel like to wear a coat like that.

I shuffled my numbed feet to my desk and sat quietly, waiting for school to start. The other girls giggled together, their ringlet curls bouncing around their faces, cheeks pink from the cold. I supposed mine were pink also, but to me their faces glowed.

Suddenly, Mrs. Massey was a warm presence at my side, whispering in my ear.

"When you smile, your eyes twinkle more than anyone else's in class, Liddy."

She patted my shoulder then stood up and brought the class to attention. Oh, how I loved what she said. I knew the church spoke against vanity but I thought this was the kind of beauty God would allow.

Months passed, and when it seemed like it would never warm up, the golden sun and showers of rain finally brought out the buds, and the grass began to show itself again. It seemed this had been the longest winter of my life. With the blink of an eye, the heavens poured down all the color that had been hiding all winter and spring. Bright blue sky, trees flourishing with green, and blossoms popping up everywhere, boasting unique colors of their own. Most importantly, the birds were back, doing their own boasting as they led their newly-hatched babies in a chorus of songs. I missed my little place behind the bushes at our old house. I loved watching and listening for birds in that secret little spot. I didn't tell anyone about it for fear of not having something to myself. I couldn't find any place like it here.

Over time, though, we made memories in our new home. We'd had an Easter egg race, laughing as we chased the brightly colored eggs down the hill. Uncle Adam played some tunes for us on the handsaw and we children all jumped around enjoying the twanging and warping sounds. My brothers made mud pies almost daily through the April showers, and although they were constantly dirty, at least they were occupied and happy. In all things, God had continued to provide.

I always greeted the changing of seasons with joy, but because of the move and the winter and spring feeling extra long, summer brought with it the excitement of Christmas. Now, instead of rubbing away the frost on the window in the mornings, I'd hear birdsong floating just beyond my bedroom window, telling me it was time.

One summer day I walked back from gathering tea leaves and berries, whistling the tunes I heard the birds chirping. Things were good and I felt happy. Memm was going to teach me to make *dompf gnepp* that afternoon, and my mouth watered at the thought. The soft bread covered with fruit and milk was a family favorite and a rarity.

My dusty feet got to the steps when I heard an awful commotion coming from the barn. Startled, I nearly dumped my entire bucket of berries. I heard screaming, yelling, and cracking wood. The voice sounded like John Hostetler, our landlord and preacher at church. The racket grew so loud, I was afraid the barn would topple over right in front of my eyes. I set down my buckets and cautiously moved toward the barn. A whoosh of dust flew out of the door, followed by a loud angry snort and I jumped again.

Dat poked his head out of the barn. "Liddy! Go to the house. Don't let anyone come to the barn unless you hear us calling. Now go."

This was an instance where Dat would not have to ask twice for obedience. I spun around so fast I made my own cloud of dust. I gathered back up my bucket of berries and bag of tea leaves and ran inside where all of us hovered near the windows facing the barn.

Dat and John came out less than ten minutes later, although it seemed like hours. When I saw them I let out the breath I didn't even know I'd been holding. We all then herded ourselves out of the house to hear the story.

"It was that bull," Dat said, helping the limping preacher walk. "He had John pinned in the corner."

"I think he'd a killed me, if Dan here hadn't come when he did." John was still breathing heavy. "He started poking him with the pitch fork to get his attention away from me."

My dad was a hero.

Both men appeared bruised and ragged, but apparently nothing was broken. I couldn't imagine that big black thing coming at me. I think I'd just die of fear. Even now the bull was still causing a ruckus on the barn, but at least everyone was out of his pen.

Through the rest of the week during our family prayers we thanked God for His cloak of protection over us all. Not only were Dat's bruises healing nicely, he hadn't lost any work due to his injuries. We also thanked God for John's safety and that he only lost one day of work. The next time I passed by that big bull in the barn I really wanted to take that pitch fork and give him a few pokes of my own, but I'd never be even half brave enough to do that.

The late autumn sun burned dark orange and beautiful against the horizon, but all I could think about was Memm. We'd been sent over to the neighbor's house, the Peterscheims, for the night, and I was sure that Memm would have the baby while we were away.

"Liddy, come, let Billy spin you around," Tillie said, pulling at my arm.

It did look awfully fun.

Billy, our fourteen-year-old neighbor, took my hands tightly and my feet were off the ground in a flash. I shut my eyes as the world spun around me. Mark, the older of the two boys, spun Bertha at the same time. Then they put us down and told us to walk to each other. Of course, we walked in all sorts of funny ways and eventually fell over in a fit of giggles.

Despite my anxiety over Memm, I had to admit, the simple joy of spinning around the yard with my sister and our friends was refreshing. And I couldn't help but think of the food I knew their mom was making for supper. The Peterscheims didn't have a lot of money either, but they only had two children, so they had fewer mouths to feed on a regular basis. We girls had full stomachs that night, and later all four of us girls cozied up in Melinda Peterscheim's bed.

When I slept I dreamed of dinner and woke up, well after sunrise, with the smell of bacon wafting up from the kitchen. Luckily, my dad wouldn't come to get us until after breakfast.

"We have a new baby," Dat said as he walked us home.

"How's Memm?" I asked anxiously. "Is she okay?"

He gave me a knowing smile. "*Jah,* your mom is just fine." He understood her labors made me anxious. Perhaps that's why he had us sent away this time around.

"Is it a boy or girl?" We all asked at once.

"Well, what do you think?" He asked, his eyes twinkling with his secret.

"Girl! Girl!" My sisters squealed.

"It's a boy," I said, sure I was right.

"Liddy's right, it's a boy."

"What's his name?" We asked.

"We're calling him Henry."

None of us could wait another moment to meet our new brother, so we ran the rest of the way home. We all took turns cooing over baby Henry and hugging Memm. I wanted to just sit for hours with my baby brother and tell my mom all about the spinning around and how much fun we had and how much I missed her. But I knew I had a duty to the family—a job to fill. Our family had seven children now, and even though I was only eight, I was old enough to be able to run the household while Memm was laid up. I wanted her to be proud of how well I could work like her. My Aunt would be in and out to help, but I wanted to make sure to handle as much on my own as I could.

It wasn't long after Henry's birth that Dat told us exactly what I didn't want to hear. We were moving again. Our move was not under as dire circumstances this time as before, but I was still sad to go away. We wouldn't be able to ride to school with Mrs. Massey anymore, but at least we didn't have to sell all of our things this time.

As we moved I reminded myself of how God had taken care of us when I thought all was lost. Maybe this was like a bird's life—moving from one tree to the next and always singing their song no matter where they were perched.

Four

Living at the Derickson Farm (1934–1935)

Labor

THE SCENT OF beans and tomatoes tickled my nose. I dished out one healthy scoop after another to the church members who had come out to help us move. What a show it was. My heart felt soft inside, like a newborn baby feels against your chest, so warm and comfortable. For so long it had pounded like a drum from all the anxiety.

The buggy ride felt long as we headed to our new home. My body was tired but my mind raced with the excitement of seeing this farm that I'd heard so much about. As we drove I learned that we would not be attending Rose Valley Elementary any more. We would have to walk two miles to a new public school instead of just the mile to Mrs. Massey's house. I told myself that my sweet teacher was just as sad to lose me as a pupil as I was to lose her.

It seemed like hours before we finally turned into a driveway. My heart stopped at the sight of a stately white house with black shutters. It had a huge wrap-around porch and trees reaching higher than the rooftop. I was sure it would be loaded with birds come springtime. But the house itself looked so inviting and warm. I could see some lights on already; perhaps Mr. Derickson, the farm owner, had come to greet us. But the buggy trudged along on the bumpy drive.

"*Ist sell net unsah haus?*" I asked my parents.

"Oh no, Liddy," Dat told me. "That isn't our house. That's where Mr. Derickson and his family live. We're just a little farther down the drive."

I peered between Dat and Memm's shoulders through the front buggy window. The road seemed to go on and on. It was already getting dark, and the tree branches scraped along the roof of the buggy. All I could see was a barn up ahead—well-kept and much nicer than many of the barns I'd worked in. It, too, was large and stately like the house, only it was red instead of white. The road continued, and I still didn't see any other homes. Before I knew it the buggy was slowing to a stop and Dat bounced out.

"What?" was all I could think to say. "We're in front of the barn."

"You'll be pretty impressed once you see the upstairs." Dat helped Memm down as she held the sleeping baby Henry.

Memm and I looked at each other and I could sense the excitement in her eyes. I think she was as eager to see the space, too. Her face shone beautifully—glowed, even—from the busy yet happy day we'd spent among our friends. For a moment I imagined what the younger children would say about living in a barn. Surely the boys would ask to sleep in the stalls with the animals, always looking for an adventure. Dat led us upstairs, and we were amazed with what we found.

I walked around and counted the bedrooms. One. Two. Three. Four. And in the fourth was a piano that had been left. It was like a celebration. Even though our Amish church taught that we should use our voices rather than musical instruments, I knew it wouldn't be long before we would be able to plunk out a few simple songs.

"Memm, look at this kitchen," I said, running to meet her in the main living area. "And we're so high up we'll be able to see far into the field and down the road while we wash dishes."

Memm nuzzled little Henry and smiled. She looked happier and lighter than I'd seen her in so long. In my thrill, I felt taller and lighter, like I could jump as high as the wooden rafters. God brought us to this new house and we would be happy here, I could feel it.

A chorus of birds ushered in springtime and then summer with haste. The busy activity around the barn apartment lifted our spirits. Dat's job didn't pay well, but it was steady. And even Tillie and I brought home quarters now and again, earning them by helping Mr. Derickson pick black-eyed peas on the farm. We were able to keep some of the beans ourselves, as well, which was worth far more than a few quarters.

I wiped my dampened face with my apron as I did the laundry. It was a hot day, and the steam from the clothing in the boiling water radiated around me. I was heading upstairs to get a cup of cold water when a car horn began to honk wildly followed by the squealing of tires. The noise cut through the humidity like a hot knife through butter. I ran full speed toward the sounds, panicked.

I could see my sisters and brothers up ahead on the road where there had been an accident and somehow my legs began going even faster. Memm was suddenly right behind me, and together we saw Dat stand up. He held what looked like Edwin, who wasn't moving. There were two other adults walking toward us along with their children. The woman was crying.

"What happened?" I asked Tillie.

"They were speeding around the curve and when they saw us they started honking their horn. I think it startled Edwin and he ran out into the road in front of the car." Tillie could barely speak through her tears.

I was amazed with the calm spirit of my parents, not to mention how quickly they forgave the driver of the car, sending him on his way. I knew that was our way, but I was so worried about Edwin I had a more difficult time forgetting their careless speeding.

A neighbor lady took Edwin and Dat to a hospital quickly. We waited and waited at home before he arrived back telling us that Edwin would be okay, but had broken his leg. Within the next few days I made a nervous visit to my brother. I'd never gone to a hospital to see my own sibling before, and Edwin was so young. Only four. He seemed even younger, looking so small in the bed. The room was cold and uncomfortable—not at all like home. My stomach turned with the smell of Lysol and bleach in the air mixed with other odors I couldn't place.

I watched in silence as he lay there with his leg up in traction while Memm fed him spaghetti and pudding. As good as the meal looked, I was sure glad it wasn't me in a hospital bed. I couldn't believe the bravery of my little brother. He smiled at me with a mouth full of vanilla pudding, and I couldn't wait to have him home with the rest of the family.

Taking care of Edwin added extra responsibilities, making the hot summer days seem endless. His cast extended from his waist to his toes, and he often complained of the heat. We would take turns fanning him as if he was royalty, like the princes I'd seen pictured in books at school.

On one particular September day the kitchen felt even hotter with the rush of preparing for company— a visiting preacher and his family. I was in the middle of helping Memm prepare salmon patties; we always had the same tasty meal with company. My mouth watered with the smells mixing together, especially my mom's baked beans, which were a favorite of mine. We'd also get mashed potatoes and chicken gravy, applesauce, and potato salad. So many dishes, it was better than Christmas. Tonight it was also my job to make the one-egg cake. Though we didn't have any frosting, I couldn't remember the last time we'd had such a treat. I guess the last time we had company— easily months ago. Now that school had started we'd probably get even less.

We did, however, have occasional visitors that would drop by between mealtimes. The adults pitied Edwin so much that many of them gave him a coin or two—mostly pennies but sometimes he received nickels and once even a dime. He proudly put them all in a little pouch made from an old stocking, though he was too little to truly keep track of how much was inside.

I, on the other hand, knew that after the company we'd just fed, he still had thirty-eight cents. When everyone else was occupied I carefully emptied the contents of the little bag into the palm of my hand. He had one dime, three nickels, and thirteen pennies. I loved the weight of them. I counted them several times, eyeballing the shiniest of them, the silver new-looking dime. I studied it, examined the ridges around the edges thinking the profile of the man on its head was so fine and nice. How enjoyable it would be to join the other students to the corner store near school tomorrow. I'd never been able to buy even a penny candy. A whole dime would buy more than I could even imagine.

A dime missing would go noticed, I was sure. But one less nickel—even the dullest one—would likely be overlooked. Right?

I replaced all the coins in the pouch then looked around the room. The younger kids were already in bed and my sisters were playing with the visiting children. No one was watching me.

As quick as a wink I took the nickel and slid it into my stocking. I replaced the pouch where Edwin kept it and secretly prayed my thievery would go unnoticed.

The next day I ran alongside my classmates with Edwin's nickel—my nickel—in hand. I thought it would feel heavy in my hand from the guilt of stealing it, but I was surprised with how merry I felt. I was proud when I handed the coin to the store clerk. I made sure to eat all the candy I'd bought before I returned to school, leaving no evidence to be found.

For several days to follow I wondered if someone would notice, but when no one did, the guilt began to burden me. Edwin got several more coins before his cast came off, and though I wasn't sure, I think my parents ended up using the rest of his coins to help pay for groceries. Though I felt awfully ashamed for having taken the nickel, knowing it could've been used for food, I kept it to myself. For several nights, however, I prayed that my secret sin would be forgiven.

When the time came to remove Edwin's cast, Dat soaked and removed it himself instead of taking him into the doctor's office. We were all excited to have our Edwin back, but our hopes deflated when we realized all he could do was crawl The doctor said he would slowly learn to walk again as his legs grew stronger, and Edwin was too good-natured to be impatient with his own healing. He played with small toys on the kitchen floor with little Henry, and any time I'd pat his dark hair he gave me the sweetest smile. He looked like Dat, and I thought that was so special. I hoped someday to have a little boy who looked just like my husband.

Hm, whom would I marry? There weren't any boys in my church that I thought I'd like to grow up and marry. They were far too rough and boisterous. I thought I would rather like a husband like Dat. Quiet and serious and sensitive. Yes. I would marry a man just like my dad. These boys didn't seem to even know what serious meant. And besides, I preferred curly hair to straight, like mine and Dat's. None of them had our curls.

Tillie interrupted my reverie when she began leading the kids around with homemade instruments and pulled me to join in. I took a saucepan and hit a wooden spoon against it. For a few minutes I let my responsibilities wait while we kids marched around the kitchen, playing our pretend music. Memm smiled as we took a little break, and she even bounced a little herself when we marched nearby. I loved the way her eyes were always so kind. I wanted to be a mother like her someday.

Five

Difficult Good-byes

I CLENCHED MY jaw as I plunged my hands into the nearly boiling water to scrub our clothes on the washboard. Like a stream's winding path, the combination of water and harsh soap surged into the crevasses of my hands. It was harvest, and every chance we older children got we were out in the fields gathering up the potatoes to sell. Digging through the dry soil and pulling at the potatoes didn't seem like hard work at first, but doing it every evening after school and all day on Saturdays wasn't just tiring and tedious, it was painful to our young hands. At school, my stiff hand could barely close around my pencil.

I told myself it would all be worthwhile in the end when the harvested crop brought in the money we needed. I didn't know much about sharecropping, but I knew we were desperate for a good harvest. Dat had gone to great effort to plant well, even hiring a few hands to help prepare the potatoes for planting. The harvest, from what I was hearing, was decent and that helped me settle to sleep each night.

Except for one night, when I heard mumbling through the old thin walls of the barn apartment. My parents were discussing something important; I wish I knew what. Even though I was only nine, I could tell there was a problem. Over the next few weeks I noticed less food on the table and the milk was more watered-down than normal. When my dad used a threshing belt to repair our shoes, I knew there would be no new shoes for Christmas. Not that I expected new shoes. I had never had actual new shoes, but my toes were so tight against the front of my current pair I had to curl them up just to wear them. I didn't tell Dat though. I hated how his brow furrowed when he was burdened.

Less than a week later, the church Bishop came over after supper. Though the man was not tall nor was there any remarkable strength in his frame, he intimidated me. When he spoke his eyes would pierce right into your soul. I was sure he could see my every sin. As the thought that I was glad he was not my father crossed my mind, I cringed. I was sure he read my thoughts.

After supper was cleaned up we children were sent to one of the bedrooms so the adults could speak privately. Generally, the Bishop didn't visit unless there was a problem—disobedience against the church, some severe injury or sickness, or money issues. Knowing this made me fee far too anxious so I just watched as the younger ones played.

I was sure my parents weren't being disciplined for something. They lived such obedient and thoughtful lives and taught us to do the same. I looked around at my siblings. None of them seemed sick. Not so long ago, Henry had accidentally poured boiling water on his face and had suffered some terrible burns, but he was recovering well. So, that left money. I knew we weren't doing well, but for the church to get involved meant that our situation was much worse than even I suspected.

It was just before Christmas when I learned what had happened. Mr. Derickson, our landlord and Dat's boss, had not lived up to his side of the bargain with the sharecropping. We had no money.

One evening, past sundown, I was doing some chores in the main level of the barn while the others had gone upstairs for baths. I was tending to our horse when Dat arrived home. As I watched him get off his bike and slowly work to a standing position, I wondered how long he'd been riding. He'd gone to peddling bundles of Crow's Foot and Holly around town for a little extra money.

"How did it go today?" I asked him, trying to sound cheerful.

"A little better than yesterday."

"Enough to—" I stopped, unsure with how to finish the sentence. Enough to feed us? Enough to keep the Bishop from visiting again? Enough to, enough to, enough to—

"God knows," he said soberly. "He'll take care of us."

By week's end I learned two things were about to happen. My dad found work elsewhere so we were moving again. We would live about eight miles outside of Dover this time. It was called Blackbottom. I imagined living in some type of deep, dark pit.

The second thing, in my opinion, was worse than living in a deep, dark pit. It made me feel like a tractor was sitting on top of my heart, leaving me breathless and hopeless. We were being split up. Several of my siblings were going to be living with other families. What I couldn't really understand was if the heart was really just an organ, why did it have to hurt when we were sad? How did that work? Why did God design our bodies that way? Shouldn't our hearts be stronger than sadness? I didn't want to hurt. I would rather be poor and eat less if it meant I could have all of my brothers and sisters around me.

Then it occurred to me that maybe I would be farmed out. I began forcing myself to be even more productive. Scrubbing harder, working faster, making every piece of silverware shine. I'd wake up earlier and come home from school quicker in hopes my extra efforts would keep me at home.

I am not sure if that's why my parents kept me at home, but it wasn't long after Christmas, when we'd lived at Blackbottom for only a short time, that I said good-bye to my brother Albert who went to live with Uncle John and Aunt Mary. He wasn't gone long, and when he returned, Edwin went in his place. I suppose my dad could use Albert's help more. Edwin was still so young and would cry when he would have to leave from a short visit with us. So would Memm. Then so would the rest of us. It was terribly sad.

The guilt weighed heavy over me when I learned that Tillie would also be leaving our home. Had my selfish prayers kept me home and pushed Tillie out? My stomach swirled with nausea with the thought. Tillie went to Uncle Amos and Aunt Mollie's. Though she would miss living at home, they were wonderful people, but they lived in another church district. This meant we wouldn't even see Tillie on church Sundays. She would, however, attend Rose Valley School and have Mrs. Massey for a teacher again. I was glad for her in that at least. It ever so slightly relieved the shame I felt for being so glad that I had been chosen to stay.

Life at Blackbottom was sad. It seemed we were always looking around for Tillie and Edwin before realizing they didn't live with us anymore. I knew that my parents felt an obligation to take the Amish church's suggestion because the church was helping us financially, but I can only imagine it was one of the most difficult decisions my parents made.

Late at night when I was supposed to be sleeping I would think about what I could do the next day to make my parents feel better. I never complained about being hungry and I'd make sure the other children didn't either. I would thank Dat for the shoes I'd been given. I'd so often gone without, it didn't matter that they were men's sized nine shoes. I tied a string around my shoes to keep them from falling off, though most of the time I just had to curl my toes.

I prayed that the chickens we'd been given from a few church members would lay lots of eggs and be fatter than ever when butchering time came. We had to make the meat last as long as possible.

But even when Tillie and Edwin were away, life had to continue. We still sang and had a time of daily prayer together. My family remained close and loving toward one another. Even as the year was nearly unmoving we had made it. At Christmas Tillie and Edwin came home for a longer visit and the homecoming was welcomed with zeal. I felt like doing a dance as they walked back into our small two-story farmhouse with their little bags.

"Here, let me take it." I took the bag from Tillie and took her to our room. How happy my little sister looked. We were so close in age; it felt strange not to have her around for all those months.

We had the whole family together again for Christmas. It was a special time, even though we only received a piece of fruit and a pair of socks for gifts. I still felt like the richest girl in Dover.

Six

Living at the Stolzfus Farm (1936–1938)

A Little Girl gets Bullied

EVERYTHING AROUND WAS frozen solid and it was still getting colder. I held my shawl tighter around my thin coat but it wasn't enough. I was an icicle. My white-knuckled hand froze around the handle of my lunch bucket. Even the wire handle was beginning to freeze against the tin pail. I stopped and set it down, painfully uncurling my fingers, finding some relief when I rubbed my numb hands together and blew on them. When I started walking again I alternated hands between holding my lunch pail and getting wrapped warmly in my shawl. On days like this I wished my coat had outside pockets.

My hands weren't alone in being cold. I had no shoes. I had gone through seasons of not having shoes—we all had, even my parents. Complaining about it was not an option, and somewhere along the line I'd grown accustomed to cold feet. The soles of my feet were like leather, and it was only in the bitterest of cold when I'd remember that I had no shoes. Today was that kind of day.

Gray icy clouds rolled in the heavens above me. Snow was coming soon, and if I didn't hurry, I was sure to get stuck in a blizzard. It was already mid-morning; all the other pupils were in the middle of their lessons and I was still walking.

I hated missing school, but since we'd moved from Blackbottom to the Stolzfus farm, I was responsible for baking twenty-five pounds of flour into bread on Monday mornings to be sold throughout the week. Then on Tuesday mornings I did our laundry. I was thrilled to have Mrs. Massey as a teacher again, so I didn't complain about the extra responsibilities. I also got to see Tillie, since she was still living with our aunt and uncle. Sometimes I'd run most of the two-and-a-half miles, making me a great runner for field days. But when the mornings grew colder and the seasons moved from fall to winter, it seemed my legs just wouldn't move fast enough to run. It didn't matter; when the snow came, both walking and running would be unbearable.

I looked over to the left and considered cutting through the pasture. It would shorten the walk significantly, though I was awfully afraid of the huge brown bull inside the fencing. He was an ornery thing, and the boys I typically walked with would tease him, making him even angrier. The bull would make all sorts of ruckus, snorting and digging his hooves into the ground. He would run right at us and stop just before hitting the barbed wire.

I stood outside the fence and looked as far as I could see. I didn't see the bull anywhere. My toes wiggled as if daring me to go. My heart thudded. Not only was I afraid of the bull, but also I was nervous about walking through someone else's land without permission. Then the thought of being in my nearly warm classroom forced me between the top and middle barbed wire before I realized it. My bucket rattled against a barb and made a tinny sound. It was the only sound I could hear, outside of the wind rustling the leaves around the ground.

Once inside, I scanned the open field and I still saw nothing. My eyes squinted against the stiff breeze that began to grow stronger and colder. I started walking, briskly against the gusts to cross the pasture. After some running and half-walking I came near to the edge of one and the beginning of another field. The bounce in my run caused my bucket to swing back and forth just enough to throw out my bread. I stopped, and as I bent down to pick it up I heard hooves approaching. I didn't wait to look behind me. I just ran, leaving my precious slice of bread in the dirt.

My legs moved faster than I thought possible and I got to the fence quickly. I threw myself all the way on the ground and rolled underneath and got up in one quick motion. My head spun to see the bull charging at top speed. His angry bellows grew louder and he didn't seem to notice that he was closing in on the barbed wire. I also noticed a nearby section that was collapsed from a downed tree, making the entire fence more vulnerable. How easily could the bull get through?

I didn't want to wait to find out, and my legs didn't hesitate as I continued running. I jumped over holes and large rocks. My ears filled with sounds of the bull crashing and snorting, seemingly part from pain and part from madness. I glanced behind me to see that the big brown beast had indeed found the downed section of fence. He had gotten himself caught briefly in the barbs before pulling loose, which made him madder than ever. Now he wasn't the only one making noise. My frightened screams rang in my ears, jarring all my senses to action.

The other side of the fence was visible now, but it seemed so far away. I was out of breath, had lost my bread, and my legs felt like they would give out at any moment. The bull snorted behind me, making me run even faster. When the pounding of the hooves grew louder I couldn't resist turning my head. I didn't just see one bull, but two. My panic heightened and I screamed into the wind that whipped at my face.

I forced my legs to go faster. The more I ran the less I could feel the bottoms of my feet. Who would have thought I would be glad for numb feet?

When I came to the third field, I threw myself on the ground again and rolled under the barbed wire. I breathed a quick breath before jumping up. Neither bull was slowing down. Would they really break through the barbed wire of this third field? I couldn't wait around to find out.

At last I saw the small dirt road up ahead and thanked God for a narrow field. Unfortunately, in the split second I took to look toward the road I didn't see the large hole. My knees buckled and I fell with a thud, twisting my ankle, my face down on the frozen mud. The pain from scraped legs and taste of blood oozing from my cut lip set forth a new level of panic. I scrambled to my feet as the two bulls barreled through the barbed wire. They seemed only yards from me now as I forced myself up and half-ran, half-limped through the field. Then suddenly I heard hooves digging into the ground from my right. In the first moment, when I saw the third bull, I felt like I was living in a joke that Uncle Amos would repeat over and over for years. A solitary frightened sob escaped my lips when I saw the third bull kicking a hoof against the hard ground, snorting at me. He looked angry already, so what would he do when he saw there were two other bulls in his field?

The three bulls seemed to have one singular thought—chasing me. I cried out in pain as I stepped on my sprained ankle but I wouldn't let the tenderness stop me. My lungs were on fire and frozen all at once when I threw myself down onto the frigid ground to roll out of the final field. I rolled into the ditch of the small road and listened for the hooves to slow down. I hoped the bulls would make one another angry enough instead of worrying about me, though I continued to run as fast as I could down the dirt road.

I ran for my life, still hearing the pounding behind me. I saw visions of my mom, hearing of my death of being trampled by three bulls. How anguished she would feel, and how much work I would leave behind. Tillie would have to come home and do my share of the work. I thought of how my dad would be so quiet in his sadness. His face would get longer and his lips would purse. I wondered how long it would take before they realized they had one less mouth to feed.

I am not sure when the rumbling of hooves became quieter, but as I reached the schoolhouse steps I looked back and didn't see the bulls behind me anymore. I had outrun them. I exhaled and cried.

"Liddy?" Mrs. Massey was quite a welcome sight when I stepped into the one room schoolhouse.

The expressions on the faces of my classmates said it all: I was a wreck. The skirt of my feed sack dress looked as if I'd rolled around in the mud, which I actually had. My black coat was dusty and snagged, and my black knit shawl was covered with dried leaves. My legs were scratched and even bleeding in a few places. I was breathless, my face felt like a solid block of ice, and I was still tasting blood.

"I was chased by three bulls." I heard myself say in the perfectly silent room.

No one said a word. I thought that if I hadn't just experienced it, I wouldn't believe me either. Mrs. Massey just ushered me to my desk and offered me her wet hankie and small compact mirror to clean up.

Later, at lunch, my little sister Bertha and I ate together. I thought about my slice of bread lost in the field but thanked God that my jar had not met the same fate. I added snow to my jar of milk, sugar, and vanilla and made a slush, which I drank slowly. Without a thought Bertha tore her bread and gave half to me. I felt humbled, and while I didn't often cry over food, I wanted to that day.

"Were you scared?" She asked after I told her the whole story.

"*Jah!*" I said, laughing. "Henry Hershberger, it was your downed fence that started it all."

I called out to Henry as he and his friends walked by, each with a small sock of marbles in his hand. His dad owned the first bull and Henry wanted to know what happened. When I told him the whole story, he laughed.

"That dumb bull wouldn't've killed you," he scoffed, and then spit in his milk can like he had chew in his mouth before walking away.

When Memm asked about the scratches all over my legs and why my coat needed mending, she didn't question my story, knowing I was not one to lie. She felt so badly about Bertha and me not having a whole slice of bread for lunch she sliced us off a generous piece, buttered it well, and after cutting it in half, told us to sit and enjoy it. I did, taking my time and savoring the moist bites.

It seemed that every move we made, even when we resisted the changes, God still brought us to a place where we were beholden to Him. I thanked God for saving me from the bulls that day. I knew I could never recall all the times God spared us from harm or illness. Though with my ankle throbbing as complete exhaustion set in, I knew I'd always remember the day I outran three bulls.

The bulls had given me enough excitement to last me through the winter, but our family was in for a long season. At first, when Henry got sick, Memm thought it might just be a bad cold. When he was unable to sit up or even eat and drink, everyone was concerned.

It seemed from one day to the next that he was on the brink of death. Pneumonia took over our lives. None of us children were allowed in the room when they shaved his head. Memm brought his curls out in her hands and I wanted to keep them forever—just in case Henry died. Everyone spoke in hushed voices.

"Can I feed him?" I whispered to Memm as she put blackberry juice and water in a bottle. Even though he was three-and-a-half, he was like a baby again, tiny and completely helpless.

"I know you want to help," she said. Her eyes looked so tired from all the sleepless nights. "But the doctor doesn't want any children in there."

That night Henry couldn't even drink from the bottle. He was getting worse and deteriorating quickly. My parents decided to have a second English doctor look in on him. Perhaps he would have some ideas.

I remember waiting by the door until the doctor came. He was a tall, older man with friendly eyes. He carried a black bag and his lips were pursed when I opened the door.

Without a word, I showed him to Henry's room where both my parents were kneeling with their heads bowed low in prayer.

It was already very late and my siblings were sleeping. I stayed awake and made sure my parents and the doctor had enough tea or coffee. I fell asleep in a chair for a while, waking up when I heard footsteps come from the hall. Dat walked toward me, weeping.

"Dat?" I stood, wiping my eyes, forcing myself awake. "Is he—" I couldn't finish my sentence.

Dat's face was long and his lips quivered for a moment as he blew his nose in his white hankie. It seemed like forever before he answered my question.

"No," he finally said. "But, the doctor doesn't think he'll make it till morning. He's praying at his bedside now."

I don't remember sleeping any more for the rest of the night but brought my request to God. Please, don't let Henry die. I repeated it over and over. No one close to me had ever died. Not really. Mrs. Massey's brother died a year or so earlier, but I didn't really know him. Sometimes one of the elderly or even a child from our church died, but no one I was truly close with. I knew that throughout life I would experience death, but I pleaded with God to spare little Henry.

My vigil had been worth the sleeplessness. The next morning as I put more water on for tea, the doctor came from the bedroom, saying that Henry was making some improvement. The small sliver of hope put a bounce in my step. Henry continued to improve but our family was not free from illness yet. Gideon, who was just younger than Henry, contracted tuberculosis in his bones. Henry slowly began to gain his strength, but it would be months and months before Gideon walked again.

In the midst of the turmoil, however, I got my wish. Memm had a baby girl. Her name was Lena, after my Great Aunt Lena, who was able to visit soon after the birth to meet her namesake.

"She sure looks like Lee with all that curly hair," my aunt said. She also helped Memm figure out why baby Lena cried constantly. Once she started adding Alberta dry cereal to Lena's bottle, Memm felt hopeful. Lena grew less fussy and began gaining weight. After the scare with Henry and then Gideon, I was so afraid that the burden would land on Lena and that we would end up losing her. But my parents were so confident in God's plan. They did not speak of their fears nor wear their anxieties like articles of clothing. They carried their burdens to God in prayer, so I did the same.

There was never a dull moment living at the Stolzfus farm. Through the summer I helped sell vegetables and prepare food that Dat would peddle in town. I imagined that the doctor's bills for Henry and Gideon had made money even tighter, but somehow we were still handling it all well enough to get by. Even though things weren't good with money and Tillie still lived with another family, I felt like we had settled into a good routine when the news came.

Dat's job fell through, as all the others had. Time to look for new work.

Moving again.

Seven

Living in Morris Corner, Delaware (1938–1939)

The Blessings of Skim Milk

MY BREATH was a white puff in front of me as I stepped outside. I put down the laundry basket, readjusted my headscarf and rubbed my hands together for warmth before picking it up again. My toes stiffened in my old shoes as I started making my way down from our small farmhouse. Dat had left before the sun was up that morning to go work at a nearby farm for the day. I wondered what he would be doing. His day work had become especially slow our second winter at Morris Corner. There was only so much wood to chop and fence line to clean up.

I stepped carefully down the porch steps. I didn't feel confident stepping on the ice in my worn brown shoes that were far too big. I was glad to get to the bottom and hear the snow crunching beneath my feet.

I knew it wouldn't be long, however, before my feet would freeze.

I was heading to the Bensons to drop off their laundry. It was hard enough work doing my family's laundry, but when our cow stopped giving milk we started doing the neighbor's laundry to pay for milk from their dairy farm. We were paid in two quarts of skim milk every other morning.

The milk mostly went to feed baby Betty, but we also used it in its most watered-down state for meals. It was a blessing to have this arrangement, even though the extra work made me late for school.

During the hot days of the summer, I thought I'd faint from the steam from the boiling water. I'd leave the enclosed porch door open, and by the time I was done I was soaked down to my waist with steam and sweat. But in the wintertime, the hot steam was welcomed. The severe cold air, however, chapped my hands and arms. My skin no longer looked like that of a girl of twelve, but someone even older than my mom.

I hopped on the small sled Dat had built for me. It was harnessed to our old mare, Babe, and made the distance over to the Benson's house with all their laundry much quicker. I whistled a tune to keep my mind from the cold, but my chapped lips wouldn't cooperate, and the sound dulled as soon as it escaped my mouth. As I gave up, I focused on getting this chore done so I could get to school. I attended Green

Hill Amish School now—a four-mile walk. I didn't enjoy this school like Rose Valley, but it was a welcome relief from chores.

Our teacher wasn't as tender and sweet to us as Mrs. Massey had been, but she taught us well. She recently told us that a country called Poland had been invaded by Germany. I didn't know much about the countries across the ocean, and as I learned more I felt like covering my ears. It was all so frightening. I didn't understand why the Jewish people were so harshly persecuted. I had never been ill-treated and I was thankful that we had our freedom. I couldn't imagine how frightened the Jews must have been.

"Hello, Lydia," Mrs. Benson poked her head out the front door before opening it all the way. After I unloaded the laundry from the sled she ushered me in quickly. She took the laundry from me right away so I could warm up. "You're a perfect icicle."

"It's freezing." Shivering, I rubbed my hands together, as I walked to the wooden stove to warm them for a moment.

They had a nice house. Comfortable and warm. The Bensons were English, and while they were not well-to-do, they seemed to live well. They were always generous and friendly toward my family.

"Mr. Benson set the milk out for you already," she pointed to the back porch. "But take your time to warm your hands as long as you need. Would you warm these over the stove as well?"

Mrs. Benson handed me a pair of bright yellow gloves. I took them from her and the softness against my dry, rough hands felt luxurious. I stroked them over the wood stove and touched the warmed sides to my cheeks, wondering if they looked as chapped as they felt.

For a few extra moments, I took in the smoothness and beauty of the gloves before I handed them back to Mrs. Benson. "Here you are. They're warm now." I felt the regret of returning them in my heart and prayed she couldn't hear it in my voice.

"I'd like you to have them, Lydia." Her smile was as warm as the heat that rose from the wood stove. "You are such a hard worker. You deserve them."

"Oh, I couldn't," I said as I held the gloves in my hands. They almost seemed to be calling to me and telling me to put them on. I looked down at them as I refused the generous gift, hoping that she wouldn't let me return them, yet still not wanting her to recognize the longing in my eyes. Oh, how I wanted to keep them.

"You must." She took them from me and began fitting them on my hands, pulling my coat over the edges to keep me even warmer. "They are as bright as the sun. The color alone will make you warmer."

"Thank you, Mrs. Benson," I said. I felt the tightness of my dry skin as my smile stretched from ear to ear. "This is probably the nicest gift anyone has ever given me, except for my parents."

"Tell your mother hello and give your baby sister a kiss for me," she said, patting my arm before returning to the kitchen.

I felt a rush of excitement and joy as I left the warm house. If the cold hadn't been so bitter as I went to retrieve the milk, I would've cried over my new and wonderful gloves.

I got on my knees near the jug of milk. Before I had my gloves, I'd always run my hands over the smooth glass surface, feeling the warmth from the milk radiate through. I didn't have to do that today. The white cream was thick at the top, the whiteness fading as my eyes trailed down to the spigot at the base of the large jar.

When I picked up the first quart jar, it began to slide through my slippery gloved hand and I nearly dropped it. Even if for a few minutes, I was sad to have to take off my gloves to fill the jars with milk. Milk was precious and I would feel terrible if I spilled even a drop. After a few minutes the jars were filled. My hands were warm again, and after I returned home on the sled, I ran the whole way to school. The excitement brewing kept me from slowing down. Even my feet felt warmer for the gloves on my hands. The generosity of good people could cause such comfort; it made me forget all about the war half a world away. God always did provide, didn't He? Was this the great gain the Bible talked about when proving your contentment in all things?

The joy of my new yellow gloves was short lived. My body ached and I could barely straighten my back when I worked in the kitchen. Having a day that moved quickly because of all the work that needed to be done became a good distraction for how I felt.

"Do you have your pains again?" Memm asked me.

She could just look at my face and know that I was hurting. We didn't know why I had so much abdominal pain. Sometimes I would curl up with a hot water bottle at my stomach and that would help for a time. The doctors figured it was probably an issue with my nerves and anxiety.

"Yes, but I'm fine." Sometimes ignoring them was better than trying to figure out why I had them to begin with. "Dat already ate?"

"Yes." Memm sighed. "I didn't have much for him. Just a little warm milk over bread. I know he left hungry."

"I'll get the kids fed," I told my mom. "We can have what's left."

Our eyes didn't meet. We knew there would be nothing left. This had become our routine for much of the winter, and I wasn't sure how much longer we could do it. I was already as slight as I could possibly be. How much skinnier could I get? These days I prayed that we'd somehow get manna from the sky. We were all hungry. No one was exempt.

"How's Tillie?" Memm asked. She knew I kept up with her now that we were at the same school again. We were not in the same church district, however, so my parents did not often see her.

"She's good. She said Uncle Amos is going to buy a farm in Kenton." I knew Memm just wanted to change the subject from our hunger. "She feels sad for us. They have plenty of food."

It made me sad, too. Uncle Amos had offered several times to help feed the family. We occasionally accepted a butchered chicken, but they were already housing and feeding Tillie. What more could we ask of them?

Later that day, Dat came home from work with his beard looking like Santa Claus from the snow, but he had a smile on his face and was singing as he bounded into the house.

"K-k-k-Katie, beautiful Katie, you're the only one that I adore…"

He took Memm's hands and spun her around several times as I looked on with glee.

"When the m-moon shines, O're the c-cow shed, I'll be waiting at the k-k-kitchen door."

"Oh Dan, what is all the fuss?" Memm blushed while the children came in from the other room squealing with delight over Dat's singing. We hadn't heard Dat sing the Katie Song in a long time and it was a favorite among us children especially.

"We've been given a cow," he told us all. Memm and I looked at each other, and I was speechless for several long moments. She hugged Dat then sent him to wash up and warm up before our meager supper.

"We're getting a cow." I hopped up and down like a child. "I wish I could just dance around the room, I'm so happy. Oh, Memm, I remember you telling us once that you learned how to do a tap dance at a barn dance when you were a girl. Will you show us?"

"Ach, Liddy, you know we don't dance." While she waved her hand to push the thought away, a smile played over her face. I knew with a little pestering she'd probably show us.

"Please," I said, urging the little ones to also ask. "Just this once."

We all stood in a line, looking hopeful. Even baby Betty seemed to know there was excitement in the air as Bertha bounced her up and down.

Memm looked back and forth between several of us and finally giggled a little as she hung her head bashfully. "All right, just this once. Step back a little and give me some room."

We moved back, leaving her most of the wooden kitchen floor as her dance space. As she lifted her white apron and gray dress just above her knees, I noticed how thin her black stockings were in this cold weather and how worn her old shoes were.

"Clap together," she called out, nodding her head to set our tempo.

Then suddenly she was like a fairy, floating and tapping around the floor. I had never seen anything like it. She pranced around like a little girl and the joy on her face lifted our spirits just as much as knowing we would have fresh milk every day from our own cow.

By the time Dat came back into the room all of us were dancing and tapping around, trying to mimic our mom. Dat smiled and I think I saw him wink at Memm. She stopped breathless and went to him and they watched us joyfully parading around together. He rubbed her shoulders, as he loved to do, and she peered up at him, happy. They shared a silent moment that spoke loudly to me.

Enjoying the happy moments with my family I began singing the song that Memm always sang to tease Dat. The rest of the children joined in.

Everybody works but Father, and he sits around all day.
Feet in front of the fire, smoking his pipe of clay.
Mother takes in washing, so does sister Ann.
Everybody works around our house, but my Old Man.

The little ones tugged at Memm's apron for several days, asking her to do the tap dance one more time. She always smiled, but declined.

Though the cow provided milk for the family, food continued to be so sparse, and my stomach made all sorts of terrible sounds. So, when Dat announced that we were moving again, I was overjoyed. A change of scenery, a new situation for Dat, a regular farm job in Kenton instead of day work would be better. It couldn't get much worse. I was sure that our new home would bring all of our family members back together again.

Eight

Maid to Help

"LIDDY, YOU SHOULD eat more." My Aunt Florence scooped some noodles and chicken onto my plate and handed me buttered toast. "You're so thin."

"*Danke.*" I smiled and accepted the extra food thankfully.

Over supper Uncle Elam's family chatted about their new baby Willie and other news in their Pennsylvania community. They also briefly spoke about America going into war with Germany. I tried not to listen to the frightening talk and just savor my food. This was my first summer after finishing school, and my first time being a maid all the way in Pennsylvania. I missed my mom, but I couldn't help but enjoy my time with my Aunt and Uncle. They had a smaller family, more steady work, and more food to eat.

My first night, though, I barely slept when I realized I had left my night covering at home and had nothing to wear on my head while sleeping. I didn't want to wake my aunt. I was too embarrassed, and she just had a baby and needed all the sleep she could get. I stewed over my problem not sure what to do.

If I wore my regular covering it would be completely smashed and misshapen by morning. That was not an option. Oh, I was so tired. Traveling to Pennsylvania in a very full car where I barely had enough room to breath had exhausted me. Sleeping with a full stomach was such a rarity; I relished the idea of it. I just wanted to close my eyes but I couldn't sleep without a covering. I sat on the edge of the bed praying, but no answer came to me.

Since it was summertime, I didn't have a headscarf with me either. I only had my typical clothing: one dress and apron, nightgown, underclothes, socks and shoes. I felt my heart beating faster, knowing there was no way I would be able to stay awake all night. Wearing a covering was not a gray area, not even at night. A woman's head should always be covered in prayer and submission. Except for washing my hair, I couldn't remember any time in my life I'd gone without wearing a covering of some kind. It just didn't happen.

I sat there, thinking. I bounced my legs to keep myself awake but my head was nodding. If I fell to the floor, surely I'd wake my Aunt and Uncle whose bedroom was nearby. I might even wake the baby. I prayed again for an answer. I pleaded for one. I'll never know if the solution I found was from God or from my own weary mind, but finally I made a decision on what I could do. That night and every night until I returned home, I slept with a sock wrapped around my head, tied under my chin. I begged with God to give me grace, making a promise to Him that any other time I left home I would pack my night covering first. I slept fitfully my entire stay in Pennsylvania.

In spite of my tiredness, I woke my first full day at my Uncle's full of energy. It felt good to be able to help so much whether it was in the house or in the barn. Life was simpler away from home; I had more time to myself, which I used to write Memm several letters. I told her all about the beauty of Lancaster. The rolling hills were luscious and the green seemed greener. I told her that the girls who visited yesterday wore their dresses and coverings differently. Their sleeves and bonnets had a puff to them that seemed fancier to me. I assured her that I was proud wearing my sensible dress and covering. Sensibility was very important to Memm.

I didn't write that I thought there were a few nice-looking boys here. I would lay awake at night and, after praying forgiveness for the sock on my head, I would wonder if any of the boys noticed me. It did appear they were aware of me. Was it just because I was new? Was it because they thought I had a pretty face or that my eyes twinkled when I smiled? With that thought I'd let myself drift off to sleep.

Besides keeping Memm updated on Lancaster news, I also put my weekly wage of three dollars in the envelope, praying it would help their stomachs be as full as mine. I ran it to the mailbox like a child who didn't know the burden of skipping meals. I felt weightless—not because I was thin, but because for a few weeks the burdens were lighter and easier, almost forgotten. My month long stay seemed to fly by and baby Willie was doing well and the whole household seemed back in order. It was bittersweet to leave Lancaster, but I was glad that when I returned home I would have my night covering back.

"Do you think it's a boy or girl?" I asked Memm as we baked bread and pie to peddle in town for extra money.

"Oh, you know my guessing has never been right." She smiled and continued humming a tune from a song we always sang in church. Then she stopped and put a hand to her middle. "Hm," she said, furrowing her brow.

I was excited because, according to other times, Memm pausing to consider such movement meant the baby would be here soon, maybe even that night. It also made me sad because she would be in a great deal of pain. I hated that part. I was fourteen, and had no problems taking on the household. Of course, I would have Memm's direction while she recovered from delivery.

"Let's try to let Memm take a break now and again today," I told Tillie, who had come home for a few weeks to help prepare for the baby's arrival.

I couldn't fall asleep that night, knowing Memm was in pain. Dat came in and woke us up. Tillie would go to Aunt Mollie's where she would care for the children and Aunt Mollie came to help Memm through her labor.

"Will it be soon?" I asked, worried.

"I already called the doctor from the neighbor's house. It won't be long." Dat's voice was so quiet, I barely heard him.

I sat with Memm while Dat left to bring Aunt Mollie back. I liked sitting with her and giving her sips of cool water now and again, trying my best to be strong with her when the pains came. I rubbed her back, and she was always so kind to thank me even while her brow would furrow.

"*Danke*, Liddy," she would say so sweetly. Thank you.

When Dat and Aunt Mollie arrived, I made sure to get plenty of rags and water for the delivery. I boiled the scissors that would be used to cut the cord. I felt proud that I knew what to do but began to worry when I heard Aunt Mollie telling Memm to push before the doctor arrived. By the time he got there, baby Simon was in my mom's arms.

We heard a lot of crying during those early weeks while Memm figured out what would work for Simon's sensitive stomach, but we all were thankful for another baby. The house always ran better once Memm was recovered and able to be her energetic self again, moving smoothly around the kitchen, making us realize how much we really needed her.

"We were bombed!" My brothers came running into the house from the neighbor's.

"What?" I shrieked. My heart felt like a weight getting heavier in my chest as they went on to explain.

"The Japs bombed Pearl Harbor all the way in Hawaii," Albert told me. He was so much like Dat with his calm, quiet voice, but I could tell in his eyes that he was anxious. The neighbors were English and would keep us updated on what was happening with the war.

Now, every time I left the house I would look up in the sky, wondering if one day I would see the Japanese coming to bomb our barn.

Nine

Living in Branford, Delaware (1942–1947)

When a Mother needs Mothering

AFTER SO MANY houses, our move to Branford surprisingly felt just right. Almost expected. The new church district was a nice change. I was fifteen and only a year away from being able to attend the *Singings*, our church's Sunday evening youth gatherings. Still, I worried. What boy would want a girl who used to wear feed sacks sewn into dresses? I was desperately boney, and still occasionally had to go barefoot. I think I was most embarrassed of the holes in my stockings. I even took a black marker to my legs and colored my skin in hopes they would go unnoticed.

I hated asking Dat for anything extra even though he had regular work at a nearby farm. He also did some carpentry work. He built a milk house on our property to help cover our rental payments. I was so proud of him and believed he could build just about anything.

One blustery day Memm and I were out hanging up laundry, listening to the sounds coming from a work crew putting up a silo on our property. The carpenters were good Amish men with families, but they had the disgusting habit of chewing tobacco. Memm and I didn't say anything to each other, but I knew what she was thinking. We were so glad that Dat didn't do anything like that. My little brothers loved to sit and watch them work and laughed at jokes they didn't understand.

"Look," Henry said, "he has blackberry gum!"

"Nah," Gideon said, "it's black chaw!"

Memm and I laughed and laughed when we heard them. Those little boys brought so much mischief and joy to our family, even when we were burdened with our penniless existence. I made a special note that day of how wonderful it was to hear Memm laugh. She sounded like a songbird.

Hearing her laugh was like music since only just a few days earlier I'd found her crying. I heard weeping coming from my parent's bedroom and I went to investigate. She was sitting on her small bed with several of my brother's pants draped across her lap.

"Memm?" I asked, worried. She only cried over big things, not the trivial. "What is wrong?"

She dabbed her eyes with her hankie that had her initials KL in the corner and took a breath, composing herself.

"Look at these pants," she said, showing me. "More holes."

"I can sew the patches," I offered, thinking perhaps she just felt overwhelmed with so much work.

"We don't have anything to patch them with. I've patched over the patches already but now, there's no fabric left. I don't know what we'll use. They may just have to go to church with holes in their knees."

I put a hand on my mom's shoulder and wanted to cry with her, but I knew this was when I needed to keep silent and be strong. After all, her very presence day after day brought me strength.

A few days later the boys ended up at church wearing pants that not only had holes, but were far too short also. They didn't care much, but I knew Memm had to sacrifice her pride. But she still smiled anyway. She always did.

As I helped clean up after lunch I overheard my grandpa talking with a man visiting.

"Whose boys are those with the holes in their pants?"

I cringed. How would my grandpa answer such an embarrassing question?

"Those are my daughter's children, my grandchildren." Grandpa spoke as if he'd just been asked who had won first place in a foot race or just been baptized into the church.

"Those pants are very well ironed," the stranger said. His curious response made me proud.

Ten

Living in Branford, Delaware (November, 1942)

When Winter Comes Too Soon

THE WINDY WEATHER was making laundry day even more laborious than normal. The sheets snapped and fought me in the blustery conditions. My hands were chapped and my face was numb. With ten younger siblings, plus Memm and Dat, there was always so much laundry.

I tied my royal blue headscarf around just a little tighter and pinned the last few pairs of pants to the line. I noticed several new holes in the knees of some of the older boys' pants that would need to be patched when everything was dry. Truly the job of mending and patching never ended. I grabbed the basket and ran into the house, saying a quick prayer that it wouldn't rain. Rain always came so suddenly in Delaware and left just as quickly.

"*Bish kalt?*" Are you cold? Memm asked when I walked in shivering. A teasing expression played over her face. I couldn't help but smile back.

"*Jah!*" I exclaimed, rubbing my hands together over the wood stove. It was early November—I'd just turned sixteen a few weeks before—but it felt like the dead of winter. "Winter is on the way for sure."

"Get warm, then come to my bedroom."

I nodded, taking off my coat and headscarf, replacing it with my white covering. I tucked the loose curls of my windblown hair and pinned it secure. My hands regained their mobility when I walked through the house to my mom's room. She had organized stacks of fabric and clothing on her bed.

"I laid out some things that need mending and sewing," she said. I didn't sew much but I expected she needed me to carry the load more for her. The younger kids were growing so fast.

"The hem in Henry's pants is falling apart and Lena and Betty really need new Sunday dresses," she began. "Mary Hostetler sold me this navy fabric for a dollar and I think it will make some fine Christmas dresses for the girls."

"I'll need your help to get it just right."

"*Jah,*" she said. "I'll help, but I know you will do a good job."

"Albert and Edwin's work pants need patches again, too," I said. "I can do them when I do these. I don't know how they wear through clothes so fast."

"They are so busy working with Dat, it doesn't surprise me. I need to check also with Aunt Sylvia to see if Tillie needs a new dress. I think she needs a black one. We're going to the other district for church on Sunday and I can ask her then."

That night Memm made my favorite dish, baked beans. Her bread tasted better than ever and there was something in the way we cleaned up together that felt different. It wasn't our conversation; we did most everything quietly, as we were both very tired from a busy day. We moved so perfectly in the kitchen around and with one another, like a dance. We Amish don't dance, but I thought it a bit sweet to call our kitchen work a dance. Our motions were particular yet they smoothly complimented each other.

On Monday my parents went to Smyrna and Kenton for our rationed gas and sugar that had just come on the evening train. I took care of the household for the day and readied myself to leave the following morning. I would head to John Yoder's to work as a maid for the rest of the month.

As I packed my suitcase a knock sounded at the front door. I opened it to find Noah Miller, a neighbor, standing there. I let him in out of the cold and led him to the kitchen where my sister, Bertha, was so he could warm his hands over the stove. He shifted from one foot to another and asked about how we were doing. There was something unusual in his voice, but the question was so general, I almost didn't know how to answer him.

"Did you hear about the accident?" He said after a few minutes.

"No," I said. "It's not Memm and Dat, is it?"

"Yes," he nodded. He stuffed his hands in his pockets then pulled them out again. He couldn't seem to stand still. "It happened around seven o'clock this evening."

My heart stopped beating and the air in my lungs went heavy. Bertha and I looked at one another. Her big, round eyes stared at me.

"Are they hurt?" I asked, swallowing my urge to panic.

"Your dad has some pain. But your mom, she's," his paused a moment, "she's not hurting."

"Will they be coming home soon? Where are they?" I steadied my voice, not wanting to show fear.

"They both had to go to the hospital, something about medical rules."

I felt so relieved that Noah had heard the news and came over. I prayed that Dat's injuries weren't serious but really wanted to know more. I released a long-held breath, relieving my lungs. My hands wouldn't stop shaking so I clasped them together. I didn't want my sisters to see my fear. I needed to be strong for them.

When would I hear more? Could I go to the hospital to see him? Even though I knew Noah to be an honest man, but I sensed that there was something he wasn't telling me, but I was too frightened to ask.

Simon and Sarah Byler came over soon after Noah had arrived. Several more people dropped in and out and I thought it was rather fine of so many people to look in on us while Memm and Dat were in the hospital. It disturbed me, however, that everyone's expressions were so grave and sober. Was Dat worse off than Noah had told us? No one else said a word except in low tones as they sat in small groups around the room. I had had enough firm handshakes and diverted eyes to last a lifetime. When we had to bring in a church bench to seat everyone, I became more than just antsy. I wanted to walk to the hospital myself if I had to.

In these moments, I thought of Memm—how gracious she was with company—and knew I needed to do as she had always taught me. I continued to serve the guests weak coffee and tea. When that was done I fiddled with the newspaper on the kitchen window that kept my mom's special pink petunia warm enough, then grabbed the broom and began sweeping the floor when I couldn't sit still.

Finally, I found the courage to confront Sarah Byler.

"Why isn't Memm here? Noah Miller said she wasn't hurt. Is she with Dat at the hospital? Is he that bad?"

"Oh, Liddy, don't you know? Didn't anyone tell you?" Her eyes filled with tears. "Your mom was thrown from the buggy. She died."

Everything went black. My skin felt cold from the inside out. My heart pounded. It seemed to fall into the pit of my stomach in one moment and rise into my throat the next. I heard the broom drop and felt both heavy and weightless. I was falling and floating. It wasn't until I woke that I realized I'd fainted and been carried over to the couch in my delirium. I shook my head thinking I must not have heard her correctly. Surely Memm was not dead.

By the next day, Tuesday evening, Memm was brought to the house in the stretcher. She looked so peaceful. Her long black hair shone, and several of her dark tresses fell from the stretcher, reaching to the floor. It flowed loose and the ends were teased with curls. Without even a single gray hair, she looked so young. Her busy and fully concerned life was over now. She always had a friendly smile on her face, and I thought instantly of how much I would miss her singing, her quiet presence, and the sweet way she said Liddy.

The wake would begin the following day and two of Memm's sisters, Mollie and Mary, offered to prepare her for the viewing. Aunt Mollie sewed the burial dress, and together they dressed her and did her hair. I didn't even want the courage to help. I wanted to disappear. I buried myself as deeply into my blankets as I could, not wanting to wake up to my new reality, pretending I didn't know what was happening in the house. I didn't want to think of how my aunts were gently and tenderly taking care of their sister for the last time. It was enough just to acknowledge to myself that she was in the house, unmoving, cold, and pale, I knew I could do nothing more.

For days to follow I questioned those first few hours after Noah Miller came and told us of the accident. He already knew that Memm was gone, why couldn't he just find the courage to tell us the whole story? I pity him being the messenger of such horrifying news, but it seemed rather unfair how everything happened. I thought our friends stopped by to give their support for Dat's injuries and wait for more news. But they had come to grieve with me, though in my innocent ignorance, I had not yet begun to grieve. I must have looked so foolish to them, seemingly undeterred by the death.

A nightmare had just invaded my simple life and I wasn't sure I would make it through or ever feel whole again. The doctors did not want to let Dat come home because of how serious his injuries were. His kidneys had been significantly damaged along with so many things that I just couldn't understand. My sisters and I, and a few other women, promised good care so he could come home by Wednesday. I was devastated for him, as he was still not well enough to go to

Memm's funeral. I had to prepare myself to be a parent to my siblings at the funeral.

About an hour after Dat returned home there a knock came to the door. A tiny woman stood outside.

"Is this where Mr. Lee lives?"

"Yes." My voice felt painful in my throat.

"May I see him?"

Most of the people had already left the house where we'd been holding the three-day wake, so I let her in.

I didn't know her, but I had a strange feeling that I should let her see Dat, even though he was in so much pain. While I felt like I was living in a fog, I could instantly see the burden in the woman's eyes. They were downturned and red, much like my own. Her back hunched and she only wore a thin sweater to keep her warm, and she held her purse closely, almost as a shield. I led her over to my dad's hospital bed in the corner of the living room. She knelt down in front of the bed and began weeping uncontrollably. We all began crying.

"Mr. Lee," she finally spoke, "it was my husband that hit you and killed your wife." Her words came delicately and softly, and obviously unrehearsed. Her eyes created two hollow holes, surrounded by dark circles and tears drenched her face.

The whole room filled with the sounds of grief. Stillness and emptiness hung like cobwebs in every corner. I wanted to be filled and consumed with the pain of my loss, but misery alone could not fill the emptiness in my soul. It only made the vacancy as tangible as the black dress I wore.

"I am so sorry for what has happened." She tried to regain her composure. "I will keep you and your family in my prayers."

"We know our God—" Dat started then stopped, painfully. He paused for a moment then began again. "We know our God always has a plan and all things are in His time." His voice though more monotone and mournful than ever, rested heavily upon me. I felt its heaviness as I continued to witness the conversation. His eyes locked with the visiting lady, and I felt certain of his sincerity. They both, with almost perfect timing, began to shudder with great heaves of sorrow. For several long minutes no one spoke, but everyone cried. As the sniffling subsided an uncomfortable quietness settled over the room. I think we waited for the woman to either speak again or leave.

The woman blew her nose before awkwardly clearing her throat several times.

"I don't know if you know about my husband," the woman finally began again. I could tell she tried to keep the quiver out of her voice, perhaps in an effort to garner strength or courage. "He isn't a drunk, not really. He's a good husband, a good father." She paused for a moment and took a deep breath. "Please, don't press charges."

In my complete surprise that this woman came to plead with Dat for her husband, I somehow felt sorry for her as she began to cry again, so vulnerable to our family.

"If he goes to jail my family will have nothing. We'll have nothing."

Over the past few days I learned that the driver had tried to tell the police that Dat was driving the buggy without a lantern, which was a lie. He'd also been heard to say that he wouldn't give one red cent to my dad. The knowledge of this worked over me as I sat there. My heart seemed to beat in slow motion. I knew the church's stance on taking others to court. We didn't believe in it. But Memm was dead. A drunken man had killed my mom. Shouldn't there be some punishment for his actions? Some consequence for his guilt?

My frustrations yelled loudly in my ears, but a quiet voice calmed me. Not an audible voice, just the sensing of a voice.

And forgive us our debts, as we forgive our debtors.

"There has been enough sadness," Dat said quietly. "I won't cause any more. I won't take him to court."

The woman almost collapsed, part in sadness and part in relief, I expect. She caught herself on the hospital bed, paused, and said thank you. She left without a word or look to anyone else. We never saw her again.

And forgive us our debts, as we forgive our debtors.

I felt the words and meaning again. I took it in and believed in it with my whole heart. Acting it out would be entirely different.

The morning of the funeral came as a bright sunny day. Because news of deaths spread so quickly in our communities, over four hundred people attended. People came from all over Delaware and many other states—Pennsylvania, New York, Maryland, Iowa, Ohio, Indiana and several others. I wouldn't be able to guess how many firm and sympathetic handshakes I received that day. Ira Nissley preached part of the service. He was on a visit from Iowa and because of the funeral he extended his stay. Memm had always enjoyed his preaching so much. While I heard every word that Ira spoke, I could recall nothing. I suspect he spoke of creation and how everything has a beginning and an end. That was common.

My handkerchief was damp and crumpled in my hand. I held baby Simon in my lap even though others could have helped. I felt a great responsibility for him. He cried for Memm, not knowing what had happened. It broke my heart that he would have no memories of her.

After the preaching, a procession of buggies led the way to the gravesite. Of all the formalities, this was what I dreaded the most. How could I put Memm, my sweet little mother, in the cold ground? Wasn't it only a few days ago she was teasing me? Just last week we spoke of our Christmas plans.

I stood with my ten younger siblings next to the casket as the pallbearers opened it for us to make our final good-bye. My breath caught in my lungs and my body felt paralyzed when I saw her again.

Memm was dressed all in white, along with her cape and apron, which I believe was from her wedding day. That was our custom. No longer would her soul be tarnished with sin and pain, she would go into the next life as white as the first snow of winter. I'd never seen anyone look so pure and ready for heaven. She truly looked like an angel.

Her body told the story of the life she had lived. Her hands looked freshly worn. They'd done so much, preparing meals, harvesting food, washing dishes, mending clothes, and more. Her hands, never idle. When they weren't mothering and nurturing, they were working. The lines around her mouth and eyes were all that remained of her smile and I closed my eyes to etch it in my mind one more time. I didn't ever want to forget.

"You should touch her," my Great Aunt Lena Miller told Bertha, Tillie, and me as she approached us. She took my hand and put it on Memm's hand. "You'll be glad you did."

I was. When she didn't feel like the soft warm mom that I remembered, it made me realize that all of her sweetness, her tenderness, her wonderful motherly ways came from deep inside her soul, not just the external. And as I looked at her one last time, I had to believe that her soul was happy in heaven and that I'd see her again—someday.

The dinner was held in two homes, John Hostetler's and Alvin Kauffman's, for all four hundred people. So many people, but, oh, how alone I felt.

Later that evening we all got back home and my Uncle John and his family prepared to leave. I felt a pit of lonesomeness and emptiness deep inside. It couldn't be covered with another hug or another cry. I was sure it was there to stay.

"Is everyone going home?" I asked my Aunt Mary.

"*Jah,*" she said.

She must have recognized my look of desperation and her family stayed until morning. We were all thankful for their extended stay, but it made it no easier when they did go. The house still creaked more loudly, tasted bitter, and smelled like death. How had our lives changed so drastically in such small moments?

Because of the stress, Tillie was admitted into the hospital with severe stomach pains. She stayed there for three days. I also became rather ill. Even considering all of that, it was poor Simon—less than two years old—that caused me the most pain. He was so young and now without a mom.

It was only days later when people began talking about how we would manage on our own without Memm. They were talking of splitting us up.

"What do you want to do?" Dat asked us all. "Do any of you want to go live in different homes, or do you think we can manage here?"

"Stay together," we all agreed. No discussion was necessary. Tillie and Edwin moved back home immediately and we would all just do whatever it took to stay together.

What a struggle to be sixteen and the eldest of eleven children. I knew I would have responsibilities that I was not prepared for, but what choice did I have? What choice did any of us have? All I knew was that Memm began and ended her day with prayer. I had followed her example for years but hadn't realized until now how much I needed to lean on those prayers more than I ever thought possible. Without the strength I received through prayer I fear I would've found a corner, curled up and wished myself dead.

Memm's face was expressionless and pale, not the rosy complexion I had grown accustomed to, but pasty and unwelcoming. She was outside by the wash line. The bed sheets near her snapped in the wind and danced like ghosts. But, even

in the gusty weather, her long black curls—loose and untamed by the bun she typically wore—remained untouched. She looked at me through the window. It disturbed me. Why wasn't she inside with us? It was cold outside but she seemed unaffected by her surroundings.

I looked around at my family. Dat sat in his hickory rocker with little Simon at his feet, playing with wooden blocks.

"Look, it's Memm," I said to my sister Bertha who was suddenly near me. My voice sounded distant and echoed in our small house, confusing me.

I looked back at my mom through the window but she was gone. In a flash she was in the living room with me. My heart pounded in my chest and I looked around to see if the other members of my family were also startled. No one seemed to react.

"My baby," she said, looking down at Simon. Then she walked over to my sister and me.

"How are you?" Memm asked. Her voice rang strangely in my ears, it had always been as sweet as a song but now it sounded so far away.

"Fine." I said blankly. My mouth felt dry and my tongue like stone. I couldn't find anything else to say.

"Is Tillie okay?" Memm's eyes, though they smiled, still seemed to look right through me.

"Yes, she's in bed." I told her.

She quietly spoke to my sister Bertha and my brothers. Then she went to my dad.

"Dan, how are you making out?" Her voice did that sweet thing that every woman's does when talking to the man she loved.

"It's slowly going better," he said to her. His face weary, even his skin was ashen and dreary. He looked sad and old.

She reached down and ruffled Albert's hair.

"Help Dat and do as he says. Things will fair out," she told him as a faint smile crossed over her lips.

"I'll go now. It's so nice where I am," she said, turning to us all. Her colorless skin suddenly seemed to have a golden glow to it. I felt warmer and my heart swelled.

As quickly as she came, she left. The room felt emptier than ever, and I had a hollowness inside that I will never be able to put into words.

Oh Memm, such short sweet moments! I instantly wished I had reached out to touch her or tried to hug her or caress her hair one last time. I should've begged her to stay. Her once vibrant spirit that could move so fast and sprightly while baking or doing laundry was replaced with such deliberate gracefulness— almost angelic.

I looked back at Dat who had resumed his reading. I wanted to shake him. Did he not feel the urgency that I felt at this moment, longing for Memm to return? I still needed her. There were many things I still needed to learn.

My ears began ringing and my breathing was rapid. I scanned the living room and it began turning black, like in a tunnel, and I felt my legs grow unsteady and my lungs suffocating.

With a sudden breath in, I sat up in bed. The oil lamp on the wooden nightstand was out but a silver moon shone through the window. My sisters slept soundly, their breathing slow and rhythmic. Memm, however, was nowhere to be found. I tried for hours to return to sleep and dream in a vain attempt to recapture even just one more glimpse of her. She never returned to my dreams. I hoped it meant that she was happy in heaven and watching us from a distance. Her time here was only thirty-seven years. Her season on earth was now through.

Eleven

Living in Branford, Delaware (1942)

Making a New Normal

A LITTLE MORE than a month later it was Christmas and we were desperately trying to find our way. We all seemed to be working and living aimlessly. Some things, however, didn't change. The snow still blew in, freezing us where we stood. The morning sun still rose, even if it stayed behind bland, gray clouds. The moon still glowed yellow against the black sky at the end of a long burdensome day. It didn't seem fair. Our lives were so altered by our loss, it seemed only right that the world around us would change too. If it just stayed the same, Memm's death seemed insignificant somehow.

I lay in bed at night, trying to banish all thoughts from my mind. In the moments when I finally began to drift off I heard the front door creak and close. There were slow footsteps across the closed porch and down the three steps. I could hear my dad's familiar stride. He must be checking on something in the barn. Maybe he needed help. I was cold as I crawled out from under my blanket. Bertha turned over and pulled the covers tighter.

My shadow danced in odd shapes around me from the small candle as I tiptoed down the hall. I heard a little whimper coming one of the bedrooms.

"Mama, Mama." Little Simon's voice cut through the silence.

I moved back through the house and found my way in the darkness over to Simon. He was sitting up in bed, fussing. He didn't feel hot, but he coughed a little and had a runny nose. I cradled him as I took him downstairs where I wiped his nose and gave him a mixture of Karo syrup and warm peppermint tea to help the cough. Then I sat in an old rocking chair that had been given to us years earlier and sang to him. I tried to make my voice sound as soft and sweet as my mom's. I knew my thin body didn't feel soft and cozy like hers, but it did help my little brother. Simon soon fell asleep and I was able to put him down. I wondered how many more nights like this I would have, comforting my own siblings. Who was there to comfort me? I couldn't ask Dat; he already had so much on his shoulders. Now that his injuries had healed, he was thrown back into the real world and back to the familiar burdensome haunts of money and hunger. He didn't need to hear about my own worries and lonesomeness. I had to be strong for my siblings; they were too young to deal with my fears.

I would pray and I would keep going.

The next morning when I went outside to gather up laundry I saw Dat's footsteps in the snow, but they were going the opposite direction from the barn. I followed them from the house to the field that led to Uncle Amos and Aunt Mollie's house. Was he going there to grieve? After that day I often heard his lonely walk through the snow. I never asked him about it or told the others. I figured if he wanted us to know, he'd tell us. I could see he was grieving so hard but remained his kind and consistent self. His quiet strength kept us going.

"Hello, Betty." I heard Tillie at the door. "Liddy! Betty Clampet is here."

I wiped my soapy hands and went to the door and said hello to our neighbor. She was a nice English girl. She gave me a hug that felt unfamiliar, but sweet. She'd never hugged me before.

"How are you all doing?" she asked.

"We're fine. We're getting by." If I answered personally I knew I wouldn't be able to fight against the lump that had become a fixture in my throat.

The girl just nodded and smiled. There was a long pause before any of us spoke again.

"Do you want to sit down?" I offered. "I could get some tea?"

"Oh, no." She blew into her hands to warm them. "I just wanted to give you a message."

My sisters and I looked at each other, curious.

"The engineer of the train that goes by your house came to see my family last week. He asked about why he hadn't seen your mom waving as he passed by." She paused and shuffled her feet a little. "I told him what happened—about the accident. He wanted me to tell you that he was real sad for you and that he always looked for her waving and it broke the monotony of his day."

I wasn't sure what to say. I wanted to cry but instead I nodded and smiled. "Thank you." I finally was able to speak. "Tell him we'll start waving for him now."

When Betty left that day I was glad to know that Memm had made a difference in this stranger's life. I wondered how many others who I would never learn of were like this train engineer who had been touched by my mom's kindness. I knew I would never be able to truly fill the gap that Memm left, but I had to try where I could.

Twelve

Living in Branford, Delaware (1943)

A Lesson in Trees

I HAD NEVER questioned my commitment to the church or my family. Still, there comes a time in every young person's life where a promise should be made, a pledge. I always knew being baptized into the Amish church would be part of my future, and as the time grew closer, I felt myself mature and grow older, ready for the instruction and final steps of membership.

I had begun to go to the *Singings* around my sixteenth birthday, just before Memm died. Since then, I hadn't been in much of a mood to socialize with the other young people and went to very few singings. In the springtime, after some encouragement from Dat, I decided to start attending again. Right around this same time it was also time to attend the instructional meetings to become a member of the Amish church. This decision to move toward my membership with the church, *gmae noch gae*, was one of the most important decisions I would ever make.

Each meeting was held every other Sunday morning for four months, with the baptisms occurring toward the end of August or early September. During the singing portion of the church services, which lasted around thirty minutes, I would be in an upstairs room with the preachers and Bishop receiving instruction on what would be expected of a member of the Amish church. My only disappointment was that there were only two other young people in the classes with me.

Willie Yoder was about the skinniest boy I knew. I didn't know him well, but when we started attending membership meetings, I found him to be a nice and pleasant boy. He was quiet, though, even outside of these serious meetings, and he had an awfully short haircut that might not go over well with the Bishop.

Katie Miller was also attending. She was quieter than quiet and, I'd been told, a little simple, but a very nice, sweet girl, with a rather pretty face. She seemed thrilled to be present at each meeting and listened intently to every word.

I'd rarely had a problem with disobedience to my parents, and never against the church. These months where our behavior was especially scrutinized left me unaffected. I knew what the Ordnung—the book of rules set out by the Amish church—said because I had diligent and conscientious parents. Still, I listened intently to what the Bishop told us: stay Amish so as not to be destructive to the church body and always consider the church when my reputation was on the line. Disobedience to the church could result in a consequence as harsh as shunning, something I did not want to go near. I had known very few people who had experienced this judgement.

"You best keep your hat on when you're able," I overheard one of the youth tell Willie one evening after the singing was over. "Your hair looks awful short. Wouldn't want to get in trouble, especially while you're going after your membership."

Willie's face reddened and his hand immediately smoothed his hair as flat as possible, as if trying to make it longer.

"My cousin cut it too short," he complained.

I was glad I didn't have things like that to worry about. Since I did all my own sewing, I made sure my dress hems were long enough and that my covering wasn't too shallow, showing off too much of my hairline. I didn't want anyone to have reason to be critical of me.

It was a cool and crisp September morning as we drove the buggy the few miles to Jake Stuzman's home where church would be held that morning. It was a nice break from the humidity of the summer, and I let the refreshing temperature calm my nerves.

Before I sat down on the backless bench, I smoothed out my new black dress and white cape and apron—proper dress for baptism. I'd been tempted to wear the black dress I wore to Memm's funeral, but I knew the requirement that the dress be new. So despite our meager funds, I found a way to pay for material and make the new dress. During the baptism my black covering would be removed for a few moments, so I could not use straight pins to keep it in place. This made me extra aware of the placement of my covering on my head, making sure it was straight and only loosely tied.

Once the singing began at church, Willie, Katie, and I followed the preachers and Bishop up to an upstairs bedroom for our final instructional meeting.

"Liddy," one of the preachers approached me at the end of the meeting. "Need a word with you."

My heart suddenly felt like it was beating inside my mouth. Had I done something to offend the church?

I just nodded my head, trying not to show my anxiety.

"You need to make sure that you smooth your hair back so that it does come out from under your covering." His voice did not carry judgment. In fact, it was so casual he could've been asking me for another piece of cherry pie. Did he not understand the gravity of his words?

"What?" I didn't mean at all to be disrespectful, but I was confused. My hair was naturally curly and there was very little I could do to keep my curls from slipping out around my hairline. It was the nature of my hair. Even my mom, who was as devout to the church as one could be, had this issue when she was alive. As my concern mounted I stared into his eyes. They were void of sympathy. There was nothing but words floating between us.

"Your hair coming out of your covering is not our way," he said. His face seemed to grow longer and voice continued in its sober and pragmatic way. "You need to make sure you don't give the appearance of trying to be like the English."

Afraid I might cry, I nodded in agreement and instinctively tried to push my curls beneath my black covering.

"You can go now and take care of it." He dismissed himself and I swallowed down the lump in my throat before I returned downstairs. It seemed everyone in church, as they had just finished a song, looked over at me as I walked down the staircase alone and headed out through the side door in the kitchen. What a relief to be where no one could see me.

My hands shook as I took off my covering and, finding a clean place, I laid it down gently. The last thing I needed at this point was to enter church with a dirty *kapp*. Since I didn't have a comb I tried my best with my fingers to smooth back my hair. I had no mirror, nor did I have a memm to consult. Oh, how that would've been a comfort.

I knew in my heart I wasn't trying to stand out from the crowd and be disobedient. But hadn't God given me curls? While I had no issues with the church or the people with whom I shared my beliefs, this was difficult for me to understand. Why was something so minor of such importance that I had to feel badly about the way God created me?

I did the best I could, but I knew as my curls dried they would not behave and stay under my covering. There was little I could do about that fact.

The Bishop, Roy Nissley, was a tall man. I was sure he was the tallest among our district and perhaps those surrounding. Dat was around six feet tall, and the Bishop quite a few inches taller. He was a good man, kind and sensitive. I made note that day for the first time that he, too, had curly hair. After another preacher spoke for around thirty minutes, Roy stood to address the church, cleared his throat, and began preaching in his familiar tempo and rhythm.

His voice became fervent and intent on his message, increasing in pitch and vibrato as his emotion grew. The familiarity of his cadence comforted me.

"Just outside there is a tree that was planted years ago into the fertile ground. Its roots growing deeply and getting stronger. As it begins to grow we all see that it has grown to be a good tree, straight and sturdy. It's branches go out from it straight. There isn't a curve to be seen. Not a part of the tree that is unsound." He cleared his throat and took a quick breath. "Then there's the tree on the other side of the house that too was planted years ago. Planted with the same care and with the same intent for it to grow with strength. Oh, the grief that it is to see that this tree hasn't grown to be straight and strong. It is crooked. It's branches unsound. It would be better to be cut down and used for firewood.

You may all be thinking, preacher, why should we be burdened whether a tree is straight or crooked, and I tell you this today, man and woman and child sitting in here, you are like that tree. You are either the straight tree that humbly looks up to heaven or you aren't. And woe to the person who is the crooked tree that hovers and hangs near the world. Who doesn't see the sin in their worldly ways."

I found his analogy to be beautiful. Oh, how I wanted to be that straight tree pointing up to heaven. I never wanted my actions to pull down the church. I felt my back straighten at the thought of it. I knew that for years to come, maybe even my whole life, I would contemplate on his words when I saw any large and massive tree.

"Just as it says in the book of Acts, that everyone must repent and be baptized in the name of Jesus, and you'll receive the Holy Ghost. You must be baptized, brother and sisters, in order to grow like the straight and strong tree in the front of the house."

When it was time for the tauf, baptism, I knelt down with Willie and Katie with the eyes of our congregation on the backs of our bowed heads. Katie was to my left and Willie to my right. The Bishop's wife joined him and they both stood in front of us. I listened intently for the words I needed to respond to.

After Katie answered, the Bishop and his wife moved in front of me. I didn't look up but still I could sense that Roy Nissley's long body seemed to be truly as tall as a straight tree as I knelt so lowly in front of him.

"Do you believe that Jesus Christ is the Son of God?" the Bishop asked me.

"*Jah*," I answered without hesitation, just loudly enough for him to hear me.

Then the Bishop's wife removed my covering and for a moment I hoped that the water wouldn't be too cold before realizing I shouldn't be thinking of such things right now. The Bishop took a small cup of water and held it over my head then poured it. I felt the cool water saturate my hair, down my ears, onto my face and neck, making my dress damp around my shoulders. I felt clean, pure, and humbled in those moments.

Before I could reflect on the sensation for too long the Bishop's wife promptly returned my covering. Though it was replaced crooked, I could not take the moment to fix it. She bent down and kissed me on the lips and then took her seat again. Roy Nissley handled Willie's baptism on his own, giving him too a brotherly kiss on the lips as a final completion of the ceremony.

We then all stood and were ushered to return to our seats. Our heads still remained humbly bowed.

"Oh, my sisters and brother, you have now made a promise. You must be careful to keep this promise close to your heart and not tear down the church. See the example of Jesus Christ who never tore down God. I must believe that the other brothers and sisters around you also often, as I do, consider this promise and, in all humility, do all that we can to not bring destruction to the church."

As he finished his message he had tears running down his face. This did not happen often with the preachers, but our Bishop was particularly sensitive to his calling from the church to minister and instruct. He took his hankie and wiped his eyes and cleared his throat again as he began a long prayer over our lives as the newest members of the Amish church.

Thirteen

Living in Branford, Delaware (1943)

A Joyful Noise

AS THE SUN came out that summer my face finally turned upward, letting the warm rays give me the hug I longed for. Around the same time it seemed we came into a routine, finally. I took over most of Memm's chores and work and Tillie and Bertha did everything possible to help. Taking over duties, however, is just not the same as being a mom. I was still just the big sister.

One task I was determined to do as well as Memm was shining her pots and pans. For as long as I could remember they were as shiny as any new set from a fancy store. I'd watched her chore over the pots my whole life, scouring them every Saturday with an overused S.O.S pad. Once she was able to see her blurry reflection in return for her work, she would smile a satisfied smile and move on. Even after a long, difficult day of work, when I put away the scrubbed pots that glowed in the lantern light just as they had when Memm was here, I would smile. So often that was my first and only smile of the day.

There weren't many things I felt I did as well as Memm. And as the seasons changed and the younger kids started school again I realized how much prayer Memm must have undertaken when packing our meager lunches. While I'd packed many a lunch bucket, being responsible for what went inside as a mother brought a new sense of accountability.

Just as fervently as I went about scrubbing Memm's pots, I found ways to do the extra things she always did for us. When I was a schoolgirl, Memm almost always found a way to pack a store-bought cinnamon roll in our lunches on days when we had a special school event. It was such a treat that, especially on a play day, I would eat a few bites before my event then savor the rest of it with the knowledge that I'd just beat a bunch of boys in a foot race or was the last pupil standing in dodge ball. Now I tried to do the same for the younger kids so that they too would have memories of what Memm would've done if she were still alive. It may have been my hands preparing their lunches, but it was Memm's character that compelled me.

Though trying to have a brave face through the daily tasks of running the household, I couldn't quite keep that seemingly fearless, yet quiet courage she always displayed. One thing she never seemed to fret over was the looming thought of war. We kept hearing about boys I remembered from school who bravely took on their enlistment or draft, never to make it home alive. There were too many families without husbands, fathers, and sons. I was afraid the laws would change and force the Amish boys to go to war. We were conscientious objectors. The law allowed for the eligible Amish boys to work stateside in non-combat roles. I felt for those boys because I knew they would rather be home with their families and working with their dads, but I was beginning to understand that there was a responsibility to serve our country during these terrible times.

Even though my part was small, I always kept my ears open to hear the sirens, warning us of a blackout exercise. We were told we didn't have to hide, but we always huddled in the corner of a first floor bedroom when the sirens sounded, just in case.

As I walked inside the house I looked up at the dark sky and wondered how anyone could see any airplane, American or Japanese, in the darkness. I tried to put it out of my mind as I prepared our supper and began gathering everyone together. Dat was away working and didn't plan to make it home for dinner.

"The Japs are coming! The Japs are coming!" My brother Albert barreled through the door, slamming it shut just in time for us to hear the loud rumbling outside. It was so loud I put my hands over my ears as I shouted.

"Turn off the lanterns. Pull the curtains. Run upstairs." It felt as though the blood in veins stopped flowing, I was so afraid. The house shook with the reverberating sounds of what must have been engines from the airplanes.

I grabbed Simon, who had begun crying in the chaos, but I didn't have enough focus or belief to tell him that everything would be all right. Once I got upstairs in Dat's room I lined up all the kids in the closet, closed the door and then stood in front of it as quietly as possible. The house was still now and the roaring far away, almost undetectable. Though the pitch blackness of the room hid the visible signs of my fear, I was sure I was as pale as our bed sheets and my hands trembled. We were all too frightened to move. It seemed we stood there in the darkness for hours.

"Dat's home," Albert whispered. "Maybe he doesn't know. Should I go get him?"

I didn't say anything. I just pushed him toward the door, glad he had offered. I would have been too afraid to do it myself. I couldn't hear anything when Albert left the room and went downstairs, and I waited impatiently for the two of them to come back. Having Dat there made me feel completely protected.

I heard heavy steps come up the staircase and down the hallway. Dat held an oil lamp to light his way, his glow not reassuring in the least. I caught myself from screaming.

"Dat, turn off the light," I whispered loudly. "The Japs are coming or they were here or something."

His eyes twinkled and a grin passed over his lips.

"Why are you laughing?" I scolded Dat. "The Japs. We heard the loud plane engines."

"No, Liddy. The cows got out, making all that rumbling sound. The Japs are not coming."

He chuckled quietly, saying nothing more. As reality dawned on us children, we all began to laugh. Just like old times. The happy sounds filled my senses in a way that the horrifying rumbling never could. It rang in my ears to the corners of the room and seemed to vibrate joy everywhere, nearly lifting me off the ground. Even as the younger kids continued to giggle and bounce around, I just stood there satisfied that, finally, there was laughter filling all the empty spaces of the house. The music my soul thirsted for.

Though I may have reacted foolishly with fear, it was worth every minute of anxiety to experience the after affects with such celebration. There was chatter and smiles around the table that night, reminding me that there was still so much happiness to be had. I was also reminded that the Bible tells us to make a joyful noise unto the Lord. Our laughter that night was pure joy. God wanted us to be filled with that joyful noise, no matter our circumstances.

Fourteen

A Bad Spot

I JUMPED INTO C.J. Walter's old truck and said, "Thanks for picking me up."

His toothless mouth made a form of a smile, though it was far from appealing. This forty-something-year-old man had been driving me to the chiropractor once a month for the past three months. He was an unusual man, but willing to drive me the almost thirty miles to Wilmington for minimal cost. No matter how strange he may have been, because of a bad fall I needed ongoing care.

My chiropractor appointment went well and we were heading home. Normally I tried to make some small talk with C.J., but today he seemed even more odd than usual.

"Oh Lydia, Lydia," he sang. He went on and sang of violets and being covered with roses from head to foot. He said the tune was for me.

I felt my face grow warm, and I gripped my purse in my lap a little tighter. I tried to look around at the scenery so I wouldn't encourage any extra interaction or even simple conversation. But as I did I realized that the scenic view was different than normal. C.J. was taking a completely different way home.

"C.J., we aren't going the right way." My pulse quickened. Was this a shortcut that I didn't know? Was he maybe just confused? What should I do?

"Oh, this is just another way home," he said, not looking at me. Then he smiled awkwardly and tried to touch my hand. "You sure are a pretty girl, Lydia."

I froze. What was I supposed to do? I was almost nineteen years old but no one had ever told me what I was supposed to do when a man was being inappropriate with me. What would Dat want me to do? Oh, I wished Memm was here.

He looked over at me and puckered. "Don'tcha think maybe you could give me a nice kiss?"

My stomach turned and I was sure my face was becoming a terrible shade of green. Half of me was becoming frightened at his behavior toward me and the other half of me worried we'd end up in a car accident. So concerned with me, he wasn't watching the road.

"I will not, C.J. Walker," I scolded. "You take me home right now."

I wondered if my tough exterior would make him think that I wasn't afraid. I hoped so, because the last thing I wanted to do was kiss him. I had never kissed a man and I wasn't about to give my first kiss away to a man I cared nothing for. He was just my hired driver. I grew more concerned as he continued driving farther and farther in a completely unfamiliar direction.

He suddenly pulled the truck over and I was sure this was it. He was going to drag me out and leave me alone to find my way home. I was sure of it. Then he looked at me and shook his head.

"You sure know how to ruin a good time," he said, sounding just like a little boy who had just lost his favorite toy. "I just wanted a kiss."

"C.J. I am not going to kiss you," I said sternly. "Now, take me home."

He put the truck back into drive and turned around and went back the way we came. He didn't say another word to me the rest of the drive. I was dropped off at home shortly after safe and sound.

"How was your appointment?" Dat asked later.

"The appointment was fine," I said. "I'm done with the adjustments." I decided this wouldn't be considered lying since I really was done with the appointments if it meant driving with C.J. again.

I decided I would rather deal with my back pain than ride with C.J. again, and if I looked for another driver, Dat surely would be suspicious. I was far too embarrassed to tell him the truth about how C.J. had acted toward me. I would rather live with the back pain than tell Dat that this strange man tried to kiss me.

My nineteenth birthday snuck up on me. I was no longer the sixteen-year-old girl that Memm had left behind to take care of ten younger children and Dat. That young girl hadn't been ready to be a mother to her siblings, but God had provided the needed strength. At nineteen I felt like a different person.

The amount of times I called upon God to help me or to provide what we needed made me realize how Memm must have felt all these years. While I had felt the sting of hunger and the burden of being poor, I realized the responsibility of being Mother was still so much greater, and the duty consumed me. I was given the amazing task of raising my siblings. Of course I had Tillie and Bertha, who had also been forced to grow up too fast, but being the eldest carried a level of expectation that only other oldest daughters will ever realize.

Oh, the burdens I felt during the nights as I tried to sleep. And in the mornings, I dedicated my day to God and to serving my family, wondering if I would eventually cave from the pressures and collapse from exhaustion and fear. My anxieties were high and devoured my confidence at times.

I was continuously reminded of the joyful noise that I felt compelled to teach my siblings. Whether with true joy or not, I began my tradition of calling "Goooood Moooorning," through the house with as sweet a voice as possible. The house would begin to ring with life and activity within moments. While I wasn't always greeted with a joyful noise in return, I knew my effort to start our day out with joy had to be a good thing.

Dat always did his best, and when he was not working, he was one-hundred percent father. He did not shirk on his duties out of his own fatigue. I loved him always but after Memm died, I realized how much more I depended on him. I knew he was lonely, though and wondered if that meant that he would remarry someday. My thoughts on that were complicated and divided.

Sickness had found our house and made the younger children its nesting place. For days Tillie and I had been cleaning up vomit from the other children who were sick. It was all over the clothes, rugs, and blankets. To make matters worse, our washer had given out which meant we were doing laundry for all twelve of us on the washboard. Because of all the sickness we barely had any blankets to sleep in.

Because it was haying season we were also cooking for all the hired men amidst the family sickness. Exhaustion had taken over, and we older girls were running on pure necessity.

But one morning, a familiar groan slipped from my lips, rather than joyful good morning cheer. I felt the sensation that I'd awoken in the wrong body. Tillie and I had been caring for all our siblings who had come down with the measles and both literally had crawled on our hands and knees into bed the night before feeling ill as well. At first I was sure it was only anxiety and fatigue, but with overwhelming frustration I realized I too had gotten the measles.

"How do you feel?" Tillie moaned over to me.

"Like I've been trampled by a herd of cows," I answered. Oh, how my head ached when I spoke. I tried to turn my head to see if I could catch a glimpse of Tillie to see how sick she looked, but my neck was too stiff. "I can't turn my neck."

"Me either," Tillie answered with a thick voice.

"Mine is feeling some better," Bertha answered.

Aunt Lizzie walked into the room with cool cloths for our foreheads and some ice water. I was so thankful for all of her help.

"You both were half delirious last night," our aunt told us. "You both were talking up a storm about all sorts of foolishness." She laughed a little.

"I wasn't," I weakly insisted. "It was Tillie. She said something about being on the porch roof." We all chuckled a little then groaned at the awful sensation that wracked our bodies.

"I think I'll be able to help around the house and with the little ones today," Bertha said, sitting up slowly. Her usually neatly combed hair was in disarray around her sweet round face. When I was finally able to turn and look at Tillie, I almost had to let out another giggle. Her red hair looked like a wreath of fire. Even her freckles looked sick.

After days of resting, Tillie and I were no better, and our measles had not yet surfaced.

"We need to have them piled with blankets," my aunt said to Dat. "That's what the doctor said. It'll force the measles out. He also said to feed them ice cream."

"They are chilled to the bone with their 104 degree temperatures." I heard my dad's sobered voice. "I hope the extra blankets will help. But we don't have any money for ice cream, I'm afraid."

And he was right, especially with a washer to replace. How long would we go with having to use the washboard? I cried from the pain I felt throughout my body. Dat sat down near me and began rubbing my feet and shushed me like a child.

It was days later before we were finally able to get up and wash ourselves. To our dismay, as we combed our hair we began losing handfuls and handfuls because of the high fevers; Tillie's having reached 105 degrees. While I hoped my hair would grow back, I was thankful that we were all well again.

"Mumps," the doctor told Dat less than two weeks later.

"But they all just got over the measles," Dat told him.

"Yes, they can go hand in hand." The doctor rubbed his face, and I could see that he was tired. Perhaps he had made a lot of house calls that day. I wished I could get up and make him a cup of tea.

Once again I had to lie in bed feeling near death and let Aunt Ivy come and take care of us all. I felt like an invalid. What good was I sick in bed?

Fifteen

Living in Branford, Delaware (1946)

Step over Step

THERE WAS NOTHING inherently wrong with Lavina Hostetler. While I knew this to be true, it was still just plain difficult to see my father with another wife. And for me it meant another mother. No longer was I the step-in-mother for my siblings. It was time for me to step back and allow my stepmother to take over our household, ahead of me.

There were so many steps to this process. Outside of suddenly having a stepmother, I had stepbrothers and stepsisters. I eventually grew to love them, but the adjustment was not easy. Molly, Davey, and Lissie were all under the age of ten when they joined our family. We went from eleven kids to fourteen over night.

I was in Pennsylvania helping my Aunt Fannie and Uncle Eli with their first baby when Lavina's name came up for the first time. The baby girl, Effie, was about ten days old when Dat came to get me and take me back to Delaware.

"Liddy, would you like to have a mother again?" Dat asked me.

My back stiffened. I wasn't sure I could even imagine anyone taking my mom's place. But my heart was split in two because I wanted Dat to be happy.

He went on to tell me that the older children at home had just found out themselves. The church in Lawrence County, Pennsylvania, where Lavina was from, would be announcing their wedding that Sunday. He and I would be traveling there for the wedding on the ninth of April.

"I know Lavina could use our help to prepare," he said with a desperate kind of hope in his eyes.

I agreed. Of course I agreed. I would never let Dat down. I was torn with gladness for him and the sadness of still missing Memm.

After the wedding I drove with the truck that carried all of Lavina's things to Delaware. Dat and his new wife would follow in a week.

On the drive I had a lot of time to think. I admitted to myself that I was afraid. I wondered if my sisters and I would still sit around Dat and sing out of the hymnal, bringing my mom's memories and voice to life in the house. It would fill in all the gaps of loneliness for a few nights. Even though Dat would sometimes look sad when we sang, we knew he enjoyed the music in the house again. There were so many emotions to experience with these transitions.

I wasn't a child, though. I knew that Dat needed more than just us children. He needed companionship. I was getting to a point where I longed for that as well. I too held my eyes wide open to see if soon I would have a partner in life that I could always lean on. In my heart I wanted to believe that my mom's memory would be sufficient for my father's needs. But my head knew better.

I welcomed Lavina and her children into our home. While I was far from perfect, I did my best to find a balance between keeping our routine for the sake of the children and allowing my stepmother to have her own way of doing things. With this change in our family we also gained four more mouths to feed. More space needed. More laundry to wash. How would we get everything done each day?

Over this transition I recalled Memm telling me just to do what I can for today and not worry about tomorrow. God takes care of the sparrows; of course He will take care of me. I counted myself blessed as a lowly sparrow in God's hands because I really didn't have to worry about tomorrow. Besides, it was laundry day and Lavina had a washer.

I fanned myself as I walked into the house. The sun was shining brightly through the windows of the kitchen casting Lavina in a silhouette. Though the shape wasn't exactly the same and Lavina was a little taller, seeing the shape of a mother in the kitchen comforted me.

Memm's movements were always as smooth as a ballerina. It was just her way. Lavina's were just as quick but different, less like a dance and more like a march. I was learning that it wasn't right or wrong either way. I needed to enjoy the differences God made in us all.

"Hi," I said, waving at her as I headed to take care of my household chores.

She nodded a hello to me.

I did not envy the transition she, too was faced with. I had such a routine with the kids; many of their requests were directed at me instead of the new woman of the house. I didn't want her to take it personally; the children only did what was most comfortable for them and would adjust in their own time. I was, in fact, relieved in some ways to relinquish the responsibilities of the home to my new stepmom.

In those early months I often wondered how she handled her own grief. I never saw hints of it as our families blended into one. Her husband had died unexpectedly not long ago. She was quite a bit younger than Dat, and I couldn't imagine myself, at her age, being a widow. How devastating that had to have been.

I dripped all over the rag rugs as we ran in from the sudden storm. I laid down the boys' pants I'd just pulled from the clothes line, knowing that when the sun came out again, they'd go right back up.

"The sun was just out?" Lavina said, leaning to look outside. "How did the rain come so quickly? And without warning?"

"Oh yes," I nodded. "Give it another twenty minutes and the sun will be out."

I wasn't sure if she believed me, but that was Delaware. Just as I said, about twenty minutes later the sun was out, beaming its rays through the drops of rain that still hung on the tips of the freshly bathed leaves. The drive was full of puddles and visions of my childhood as we used to jump from puddle to puddle after such a perfect rain ran through my mind. I could almost hear our giggles. It didn't take long for the young kids to do just that. It was nice to see my brothers and sisters, full and step, playing and laughing together.

As I ran an old towel over the line, drying it, I was amazed. How could such small, delicate raindrops, suspended perfectly on a wire, have the strength to capture the sunlight? It reminded me of how a baby could laugh when fresh tears were still wet on his cheeks. It amazed me how God's creation exemplified life. Sunshine beams more radiantly when forced through even a single drop of rain. Just as happiness is felt more dearly, more deeply, after your soul was emptied with tears. Life at times was a painful joy.

Sixteen

Living in Branford, Delaware (1946)

Rum Springa

OUR COMMUNITY WAS small when it came to passing stories back and forth. I remember hearing about a girl named Martha Hostetler who wore a small barrette that sparkled beneath her bonnet, letting it peek out on the side. There also was a boy named Samuel Byler who had been caught with a radio in his buggy.

Of course, this was during their *rum springa*—running around—years, and there were more allowances given to us. While many of the Amish youth took advantage of these years, I had not been that adventurous or that interested. I felt it was disrespectful of all the sacrifices my parents had made to teach us the ways of the church. After my baptism, these temptations became less alluring. I was nearly twenty and could feel myself longing for the next season of my life.

Even with a small social circle, the district was still very spread out. We lived so far away I often couldn't attend the youth gatherings; *Singings*, on Sunday nights. A neighbor girl, Anna Coblentz, was in the same predicament. She was a little older than I and lived about two miles away. During times when we couldn't attend the Singings she and I would meet halfway between our homes and dip our feet in the brook under a little bridge. We'd talk about our families and about life. She had a stepdad; though every situation is different, she understood loss.

In my earlier years of *rum springa*, I dated often. I didn't date the same boy for too long because I hadn't found anyone I was ready to settle down with. Having a date, though, meant having a ride to and from the Singings. The Singings could easily be more than four miles one way, so this was no small issue to have a ride instead of walking. The socializing with the youth was important to me—and fun, too.

Often enough, however, I still ended up walking those miles home in the dark. One night, two men in a car stalked me. They even got a spotlight out to search for me as I rolled under the barbed wire fence of a muddy bull pasture. The passenger got out of the car to shine the light more closely. I prayed and prayed myself through my fear, and after they left I waited another fifteen minutes before I attempted to get up. I was only a mile from home and ran the rest of the way.

Another time Bertha and I hid in the ditch after we heard heavy footsteps coming closer. Someone was whistling a tune, which in the darkness, we found frightening. Once we couldn't hear anything more we went a short distance to Rudy Byler's home and stayed the night. We were too afraid to walk the remaining distance home. The next day we found out that it was Dat whistling. He had come out to walk us home. When he didn't find us, he assumed we stayed with Rudy's overnight, which happened now and again. Bertha and I felt a little foolish that we didn't recognize the tune, but the feeling passed with the comfort of knowing that Dat came looking for us.

I opened the curtain just a little more so the outdoor light would brighten up my small bedroom, holding up a small hand-held mirror my aunt had put on the dresser. Over the short years since Memm had died I'd studied the reflection more intently. I could see my eyes were her shape and I'd practice smiling to see if I could manage one as kind as hers, trying to capture the tilt of her head and the way she'd look up through the top of her eyes so sweetly. She was such a model of a good wife and mother. Oh, how I willed myself to be like her.

I put the mirror down before carefully taking the straight pins from my hair and removing the black covering I wore on Sundays. I took a small black comb and smoothed back the unruly frizzy curls that had escaped my tight bun. I would have to use some water to tame the curls that framed my face.

My hair was as dark as my mom's with a hint of auburn, and very curly. It waved from the very root even when I pulled it tight. I picked up the small mirror again and smiled with my mouth open, showing my teeth. That was definitely not right. I shook my head and tried to conjure up the image of Memm's face. It took a few extra moments to see a clear image in my mind. I considered her face, her shy smile and bashful expression in her eyes. Then opened my eyes and mimicked it as best as I could. Maybe if I'd get it just right I would meet a nice boy, get married, and my season of summer would arrive.

Seventeen

Living in Branford, Delaware (Spring, 1946)

When a Stranger Drives into Town

MATTHEW TROYER WAS a charming boy. He was handsome, with a bright smile. And he liked me. A lot. I liked him, too. His charismatic personality kept me laughing and interested. When we started dating in the spring, I welcomed his companionship like I welcomed the buds beginning to bloom.

For several months not only did I have a ride home from the Singings but I also had great company. I wasn't in love with Matthew, though, and wasn't sure how much longer we could go on simply dating and chatting without moving forward to what would naturally be the next step. As nice as he was, he wasn't the one I wanted to marry.

As I arrived to a Friday night gathering I saw a few of the regular Amish boys huddled around a car. Once I got closer I saw three boys I didn't recognize. A handsome sandy-haired boy leaning against a blue Buick got my attention. He was wearing a light blue turtleneck with Amish denim pants. The boys seemed fascinated with the car and a group of girls nearby were giggling together while peeking over.

"Barb," I asked a friend, "whose car is that? Who are those boys?"

"Oh, that's Alan Mast's car," she whispered. "He's at the CPS camp out in Maryland. I don't know the other two boys, but I heard they're from the same camp."

"Why is he here?"

"He's just visiting for the weekend," she said, her eyes still on the newcomer.

We watched as the boys talked with Alan then they all laughed out loud. I felt my temperature rise when the whole group of boys, along with Alan, came to gather under the porch of the house. I found him handsome and exciting.

Alan's wavy hair was cut differently than the typical bowl cut of other Amish boys. It feathered back away from his face. He smiled at me and I looked away. When I peeked back he looked again. He laughed and told a few stories while still looking over at me every so often. Each time our eyes met I looked away quickly and a dash of adrenaline ran through my body.

It was almost time for the Singing to start when Matthew found me.

"Liddy, I have a gift for you," he told me with a bright smile across his face. "I'll give it to you afterwards."

"You might not want to do that," I said, knowing that it wasn't right for me to lead him on. I couldn't think of anything else to say at the moment, but with Alan in town only for the weekend, I didn't want to miss my chance at a date with him. I just hoped he would ask. How could I possibly explain that to poor Matthew?

I was saved. The Singing was about to start. We went to our separate sides of the large living room since the girls and boys were not allowed to sit together. Matthew went over to his friends on the boys' side and I took my place on the girls' side with my sisters, Tillie and Bertha.

As the Singing ended everyone began to mingle and pair up to drive their buggies to the girls' home for their dates. I had been thinking about Alan and what his plans would be for the evening. I was trying to pretend I didn't notice as he mingled close to my group of girls when I heard a voice near me.

"Hello." I liked the smoothness of his voice.

I turned around quickly to see Alan standing there.

"Hi."

"I'm Al," he said with smiling eyes. "You're Lydia Lee."

I liked how he said my name. And, he spoke in English. I was thinking he must have grown accustomed to talking in English while at the Civilian Public Service Camp, so I opted for English instead of Dutch.

"Yes, I'm Lydia," I said breathlessly and I felt a shy smile creep across my face.

"Want to go for a drive?"

I looked around; the house and porch were emptying. Poor Matthew was talking with his group of friends across the way, so unsuspecting. I needed someone to tell him I was going to go with Al. I just couldn't do it myself.

"I'll meet you at your car in a minute," I told Al and watched him walk toward his car.

I found my sisters who were already planning their dates with Al's two friends who had come with him. Then I found my friend Barbara.

"Barb," I said in a whisper. "I need you to talk to Matthew."

"What for?"

"Tell him I'm going on a date with Al." I winced hearing myself say the words. I knew this would tell Matthew that I was moving on. There had to be a better way to break the news to him, but in that moment, Barbara's message to him from me would have to do.

As soon as Barbara agreed to tell Matthew, I gathered my things and skipped over to Al's car. He had the passenger side window down and looked at me. His sharp, blue eyes had a look of mischief that I recognized.

"You coming?" He said, smiling at me.

"Yep," I said, jumping in.

I enjoyed riding in the car. It was getting chilly so I kept the window up. I was so used to riding in a buggy, it felt like no time at all before we were at my house.

I didn't have anything but tea to serve him, but we had a great evening talking. We laughed and laughed. He told me of some of his duties at the Civil Public Service Camp and I was proud that so many of our Amish boys were serving with such skill and strength.

We went on another date on Sunday and then he returned to the camp. We didn't date each other again. I suppose we both knew that we weren't the right pair, even though we had a good time.

So, I kept trusting. And waiting.

Eighteen

Living in Branford, Delaware (Summer, 1946)

A Blind Date

WITHOUT A STEADY boyfriend, I went back to my humdrum days of knowing what was around every corner. It seemed there was little surprise or excitement in my life now. I pushed discontented thoughts out of my heart.

I was glad to have two especially close friends, though. Liddy Troyer, who was actually a year or so older than I, and Liddy Yoder who was the youngest of us three. We got teased relentlessly that in order to be in our club you had to be named *Liddy*, and it did make things confusing. We even had to use our last names when talking with each other. All three of us were excited to meet some new boys from outside our community.

On a particularly hot summer day, Liddy Troyer brought me some welcome news.

"You'll never guess," she said. "Remember Jake Peachy?"

I rolled my eyes. "How could I forget? I was a table waiter with him at Lizzie's wedding. He wouldn't leave me alone."

"He's at the CPS Camp in Maryland right now." My friend's eyes sparkled with excitement. "Apparently he was going on and on about you."

"Ach, well, doesn't that just beat all," I announced. "He's just a big tease and I'm not interested."

"Just hold your horses, you might be interested here in a second." She pulled a letter out. "Apparently all of Jake's stories got some Ohio boy interested in you. His name is Freeman Coblentz and he's at the camp and he wants to have a date with you."

"What?" I sat up a little straighter. "I don't know anyone named Freeman Coblentz."

"I'm supposed to answer him back and let him know if he and two other friends of his can come out and have a date with you, me, and Liddy Yoder."

I had the answer before she was even done asking. A young man I had never even met wanted to date me? Yes, I would date him. I hadn't been so thrilled about anything since Al had driven into town. I was almost twenty and a lot of girls were married by now.

I could hardly wait until I heard more from Liddy Troyer about when the boys would take the bus out here for a visit. I got permission to stay with my cousin Liddy Yoder that weekend though, since I didn't want to tell Dat about Freeman yet. All three of us girls decided not to share our plans with our parents. My grandparents lived next to cousin Liddy Yoder's house and it would be empty the night the boys came into town. We could use their house for our triple date without anyone noticing. There would be far too many rules imposed if we told anyone of our plans to meet three strange young men who had written, wanting to meet us.

The boys hid in the nearby field until it was dark enough for them to come unnoticed. All of it was so secretive I was nearly bursting with excitement. The night was thick with darkness when they arrived on the doorstep at well past nine o'clock. In fact, I couldn't clearly see any of the boys' faces. I shook with anticipation as they entered the dark house. We each had nothing more than a candle so that no one would notice the glow of lanterns coming from the house and interrupt our night.

"Hey, you girls ever heard the story about the man in the cornfield on a hot summer afternoon?" One of the boys said the moment he walked in without any of us even having a chance to introduce ourselves. He spoke quickly, like he was in a hurry. I heard laughter behind every word.

"No?" The three of us girls responded. I couldn't help but smile.

"Well, it got so hot that the corn started popping," the boy slapped on his legs, making popping sounds. "His horse thought it was snow and froze to death."

The three guys laughed as if it was the funniest joke they'd ever heard. I laughed because I found this jokester's personality magnetic, even though the joke was rather ridiculous. I hoped he was Freeman Coblentz.

"Leave it to you, Coby. You're always full of some rotten joke," one boy said.

Coby. I rolled the name around in my head. I didn't remember that any of them were called Coby. Maybe it was a nickname? Could it be short for Coblentz?

I listened to them laugh and banter at one another for a few minutes and analyzed what I expected to be Freeman's voice. It wasn't deep and bottomless like Dat's, but expressive and carried a chuckle with every word. I could hear his smile. I wouldn't be able to explain what excited me about meeting Freeman— why I found him instantly charming and somehow perfect. Perhaps it was the anticipation of his arrival that made me imagine he was truly special. Maybe it was the idea that he wanted to meet me sight unseen that made me feel truly special, too.

Once we finally made our introductions in the dark, we split off into three different parts of the house for some privacy. I was filled with anticipation as I led

Freeman through the dark house, measuring my steps. When we got to one of the couches and my eyes began to adjust to the dim glow of the candle, I could vaguely see that he was of average height and wasn't wearing Amish clothes. I couldn't see anything more, really, but imagined a wide smile. As we sat down he pulled out a flashlight and instantly began teasing me with the ray of light that was much stronger than the candle I brought.

"That flashlight sure would've made it easier to walk through the house," I bantered. The one good thing about the darkness was that he couldn't see me wring my hands or bite my lower lip, like I always did when I concentrated or felt nervous.

"It was fun watching you squirm in the dark." He said with the same laughter creeping into his voice.

I imagined him winking, though there was no way I'd ever know if he did. I could already tell that he was a tease.

We talked for hours and hours, our conversation continuing well into the night. We talked about our lives, our families and the little worlds we lived in. He told me of his war service at the Civilian Public Service camp. He worked in the morgue at the military hospital. He had the unfortunate job of having to tend to the dead sixty feet below ground; it had to be cold to keep the bodies from decomposing. He was responsible for bathing them among other tasks that I didn't even want to think about.

"Isn't it scary?" I asked. I would be petrified to be around the dead bodies of strangers all day, especially alone.

"Sure is," he admitted. "I often take a patient from the mental ward down to the morgue with me. I do make him walk in front of me, though, just in case."

While we both laughed I could sense that he was not the type to have a serious conversation for very long. He needed to interject some type of joke or change the subject. It was refreshing. Seriousness and intensity in life was all I'd ever known. His stories of adventures from outside our little community and even his corny jokes were music to my ears. Here in the dark I saw this man better than I'd seen anyone else in the light. I had never met anyone like him. His boldness alone in wanting to meet me after only hearing a few stories piqued my curiosity. Which ones had he heard? I was too nervous to ask. I couldn't explain it, but being around him made me feel removed from the years of hunger and mourning. My laughter was unforced and genuine. I suspected Memm was smiling down at us, giving me her silent approval.

As I contemplated my immediate attraction he suddenly flashed a light in my face and laughed at the expression I made.

"Freeman," I scolded playfully, "don't you do that without giving me the chance to see your face."

"You have pretty eyebrows, do you pluck them?" He teased. "I bet the rest of you is just as pretty."

I suspected another wink as I felt my face glow with a warmth that spread through the rest of my body. Now, if only I could catch a glimpse of him.

"You know, I'm heading out west," he blurted suddenly. I couldn't tell if he was teasing or not. "I'm gonna be a country-western singer once my service is through. I have already been voice-tested."

I wasn't sure what voice-tested meant but I didn't want to seem ignorant so I just went along with his story.

"Oh? When is your service completed?" I tried to sound casual in my asking, but I was so curious when he would be free to come and go as he needed without the restrictions of the CPS.

"Next month." He clapped his knee loudly and let out a little holler of excitement.

I tried to not consider that if he were serious that meant that he would go and have an adventure and leave me here. So soon was I ready to give him my heart. I hoped that he'd ask me to go too. Somehow I knew I'd go anywhere with him. I couldn't remember any time in my life where I'd laughed so hard and felt such eagerness about anyone.

Then, without warning, he leaned forward and kissed me. Though it was brief and almost startling, I reached and touched his arm. His shirt felt thicker than a typical Amish man's shirt, and he wasn't wearing suspenders, my suspicions about him not wearing Amish clothing had been correct. It exhilarated me. There was so much more to him that I wanted to know. I prayed I'd be given the chance. I prayed that if he left, he'd take me with him and if he stayed, he wanted me by his side.

We talked and shared a few more kisses before I heard one of my cousins telling me that we needed to say good night. I regretfully said good night to Freeman, wondering if at breakfast I'd even know which one of the three was the one I'd already fallen in love with.

The next morning, back at my Aunt and Uncle's house, we rushed around the kitchen before the boys arrived. My mind spun in a million directions and I thought of how different we three Liddys were. Liddy Troyer was tall and thin with dark pin-straight hair. She couldn't be confused whatsoever for Liddy Yoder who was short and shapely and very cute, maybe even too cute. What if Freeman liked a girl who was long and willowy or preferred petite and lovably attractive? I felt I was somewhere in the middle—not nearly as tall as Liddy Troyer but nowhere as shapely as Liddy Yoder. Was I cute? I never considered myself more than average. What if Freeman didn't like me once he saw me?

It had already been arranged that we girls wouldn't be attending church that Sunday morning, but we promised to attend the other district's church the following week. My aunt and uncle said it was fine as long as we promised to behave ourselves, but then they hadn't known we'd invited three strange young men to visit us. They'd been asleep by the time we sneaked to the empty house next door to wait for the boys to arrive in the dark.

Once Liddy Yoder's family left for church the three boys came over for breakfast. I instantly felt my stomach do flip-flops when they arrived. I was sure that I would faint, or worse, realize that Freeman Coblentz in the light of day was nothing like what I imagined. It's not that looks were everything, but I couldn't help having some expectations. What if my imagination of him was by far leaps and bounds better than reality?

There was a knock at the door and it seemed the heart of the house skipped a beat. We all made eye contact, and walked together toward the door. As the boys said good morning, I smiled and returned the greeting and tried not to make it obvious that I was critiquing each of them as they entered, trying to determine which one of them was Freeman. I would know by the voice had they spoken separately, but their good morning was in unison and they all wore suspicious smiles on their faces.

One of the boys was of very average height and, in my opinion, only average looking. Another was a little taller and handsome. The third was quite handsome—not overly tall, but when I looked at his eyes the blueness glimmered. His crooked smile showed off the whitest teeth I'd ever seen, highlighted all the more by his tanned skin. His hair was a light brown that showed hints of red. And he had curls, just like me. He, I knew, was Freeman.

He wore a white uniform shirt, but the collar lay open and loose. He also wore brown, store-bought pants. He glowed in the sunlight that fell on him through the window.

We all introduced ourselves again, feeling silly since we'd spent hours with the boys the night before. The other boys were Jonas and Adam, and my friends seemed pleased with whom they'd been matched. I was glad they weren't disappointed. But I knew that I had gotten the best of the three.

Freeman was by far the most talkative of the group. He cracked joke after joke. The boys also talked about the camp and how ready they were to be finished with their two-year service. I found it all so interesting. My world was so small, having traveled outside of Delaware only a few times. I considered what Freeman had said the night before about running away out west and becoming a singer. I imagined myself going with him and seeing the world—anywhere that wasn't the country roads of Delaware.

"So, what do you think?" Liddy Troyer interrupted me as I washed dishes. The guys were talking and laughing amongst themselves as we girls cleaned up.

"I hope he likes me as much as I like him." These were the only words I could find to say. Liddy jabbed me in the ribs and giggled. It was clear she felt the same way about Jonas.

We all headed out in the open Dearborn buggy after the meal and enjoyed driving around and continuing to get to know each other. Freeman and I sat in the third bench, in the rear of the runabout, relishing our time together. The horse, Bruce, was so slow that every time he slowed to a near stop Freeman would make the whoosh sound like a bus stopping. It seemed he had a joke for everything.

At the bus station I felt dizzy with joy, but so sad to see him go.

"I might write you," he teased.

He must have seen the expression of worry run across my face and he smiled sweetly.

"I promise I'll write." He kissed me. "I should be able to get a letter out about every other day."

"I'll write you back." I said, wishing he could stay forever.

"And don't you worry, Liddy, I'll be back next weekend."

He gave me another hug and a kiss and then, with a bounce in his step, he bounded on to the bus.

He'd stayed as long as possible, taking the last bus of the day. I knew he would get little sleep before his workday started in the morning. I also knew I would get little sleep because I would be thinking of Freeman Coblentz.

Nineteen

Living in Branford, Delaware (1946)

Glimpses of Summer

FREEMAN VISITED THREE weekends in a row, each time leaving me overwhelmed and completely thrilled with his ready smile, the way he glanced out of the corner of his eyes, and, of course, his corny jokes. I wished I lived at home so Dat could meet him, but I knew if we got serious enough, that day would come.

"If I asked, would you run away with me?" he said late one night on his third visit as we sat on the front porch of my uncle's house.

"Yes," I said in an instant. My heart skipped a beat.

"Well, I haven't asked you." He teased.

I gave him a playful scolding and then bravely added, "We wouldn't need a big wedding. Just our families, a small cake, a few witnesses." I couldn't believe that I offered my thoughts so openly. Dat hadn't met him yet. And, Freeman hadn't even said that he loved me.

He laughed. "Nah, we won't get married that way."

When I frowned, he gave me a quick kiss to appease me. He told me some funny story and was off on the bus back to Maryland before I knew it. Oh, this boy was under my skin and in my heart. At night I replayed his words over in my head and fell asleep smiling.

The balminess of summer ushered in September. By its close, the leaves began to change colors and fly around me as I took my daily walk to the mailbox. The mailman delivered at eleven and I was often there waiting for him. Freeman wouldn't be able to visit at all this month. I reveled in his letters that came every other day, soaking up every word. I'd read it over and over until it was nearly memorized by the time the next one would come. His letters were romantic and sweet, and he started calling me by the silliest pet name Sugar-coated Pickle. It made me giggle every time I read the funny name. It was nonsense, but I loved it. Despite the tender letters, I waited and waited for the time when he would tell me that he loved me. I wrote it in the teeniest of letters underneath the stamps on the envelopes.

"There's a letter for you," the mailman said as I trotted up to him. "Here you go." He handed me the small stack of mail for the house, my letter on top.

I opened it right away. This letter reminded me that his service would be complete in a week and he'd be returning to his parents' home in Ohio. Did thoughts about running away to become a Country Western singer still cross his mind? I secretly hoped not, afraid if he did, he would also forget about me. If he went to Ohio and settled down, maybe he would consider me as part of his future.

He visited in early October before returning to Ohio, and I counted the minutes until he arrived. I'd been good for nothing that day. Every time I saw Freeman I found him more handsome and charming than the previous visit, and I knew I'd go anywhere with this man. He'd walk up to me with a crooked smile and a twinkle in his eye, often whistling some tune or even singing "The Old Rugged Cross."

I was in love.

After the supper clean up was done and my aunt and uncle and their children were all heading for bed, Freeman and I had permission to stay up.

"Come," Freeman said, patting the space next to him on the couch. "*Huck ana.*" Sit down. "I have something for you."

He handed me a beautiful birthday card, with colorful flowers and birds on the front. I felt warm and my eyes began to brim over. When I opened it carefully, money fell into my lap.

"What is this for?" I asked, surprised.

"You need a new coat, Liddy," he said. "Look, yours is almost worn right through. It's not going to keep you warm for the winter."

"I don't know what to say." I stared at the money in my hands.

This gift spoke so loudly to me. He was looking out for my well-being and he didn't even have to yet. I was still living at home with a dad caring for me. But his thoughtfulness toward me, wanting to keep me warm, touched me more than anything he could've bought for me from the store.

"I have one more thing." He smirked. "But you'll have to come with me."

"Can we go now?" I asked as we pulled our coats on and headed to hitch up the buggy.

"*Jah*," he said. "We won't be gone long."

It wasn't much of a drive and he stopped at a little corner store. We went inside together and to my amazement he bought two pints of vanilla ice cream, one for each of us. We went back to the buggy and back to my aunt and uncle's home. Freeman had no idea that I would be able to finish my entire pint of ice cream alone. But he also had no idea that it was the first time I'd ever tasted ice cream.

"If I asked you to marry me, would you say yes?" He asked as we devoured our vanilla pints.

"Yes," I answered again. No hesitation. I loved him.

"Next month?" His eyes were twinkling.

Was he serious this time?

"Really?" The rest of the evening was a blur. I couldn't believe it. Freeman had finally proposed to me. We were getting married in November, only a little more than a month away.

He left for Ohio and I floated through my daily routine without consequence. My upcoming wedding was all I thought about. I hadn't spoken to my friends yet about the plans since I wanted to talk with Dat first, and it wasn't our way to discuss these plans openly. The church itself would only announce it two weeks before the wedding, which would be held on a Tuesday or a Thursday. Of course, once I spoke to Dat I would share the news with my sisters and close girl friends, I needed their help with the details and someone to daydream with.

I was moving back home in the next few days and it was after supper one evening when I decided to talk to Dat about the plans Freeman and I were making. Everyone else was either asleep or occupied. I wanted him to myself.

"Dat," I said sitting on the couch nearby. "Freeman asked me to marry him. We are planning to get married next month."

In my dad's typical way, he gave me a serious expression and paused for several long moments before he spoke.

"You haven't known him very long," he started. "You are sure about this?"

I nodded, my eyes locked with his.

"I don't know anything about his people. I'll want to learn more. And I'll want to talk with Lavina also. Okay?"

I nodded again, not sure what to expect.

It was the next morning while cleaning when I faced a set back that I hadn't expected.

"We'd like you to wait till March," Lavina told me. "It's just better for me and your dad."

I couldn't speak for the disappointment I felt. She and Dat were expecting their first child in February. March would be more convenient. I did my best to understand their reasons but, of course, I was sad that I'd have to wait several more months.

Discouraged, I wrote to Freeman explaining everything. It had come as such a surprise to me I had nothing to say but to agree and begin plans for a March wedding. I decided not to let the disappointment consume me and continued dreaming about my future with the man I loved. Perhaps God wanted me to spend one last Christmas at home with my family. Since Freeman and I would be living in Ohio, I did want to enjoy the time I had left with my family all under the same roof.

Freeman wrote me of his disappointment. Though it couldn't completely make up for the set back, he decided that since our wedding was delayed it would be a good idea for me to visit his family in Ohio for Thanksgiving. When thinking of meeting my future in-laws, my heart would go from racing one moment to halting all at once the next. Not only would I get the chance to meet Freeman's family, I would get my first glimpse at where my new life would be once we were married.

Freeman came to Dover to travel with me back to Ohio. While his visit to Dover was only for a little more than a day, he met my dad, stepmom, and siblings for the first time. I could feel the blood rushing through my veins with nervousness. Dat and Freeman had personalities that were different as night and day. Dat had always been strong with few words and had a quiet gentleness in his smile and eyes. Freeman was the most talkative man I knew, and his expressive face was one of his greatest charms. His eyes often gave me the impression that he was up to no good, though not in an evil or sinful way. Dat chuckled quietly. Freeman bellowed out his laughter, making his face turn bright red, slapping his knee. Dat's curly hair was often windblown and in disarray.

Freeman's was always meticulously combed and styled like an Englisher.

I decided I must rely on their similarities. Both were hard workers. Neither complained about their duties and responsibilities. I could trust both of them with my life. Most importantly, I loved them both desperately.

Despite my anxiety, the meeting went well. We had an easy meal at home, even though we still did not have enough money to make the meal especially unique. My sisters winked at me, and when Freeman wasn't looking, they'd take turns poking me in the ribs, teasing. They found Freeman as handsome as I'd described. My brothers didn't say much; they were a lot like Dat, but I could sense that they got a kick out of Freeman's free-spirited way. I often considered his name when thinking of his personality. Freeman—he sure had a freedom about him that I'd never quite seen before. It consumed me.

While my sisters, stepmother, and I cleaned up the kitchen, I listened as closely as possible to hear what they talked about over tea. I wished that I could sit for a spell and talk with them. Oh, how I wanted Dat to adore the man I loved. But working in the kitchen with my stepmom and sisters kept my nervous hands busy.

"I got your letter about marrying Liddy," Dat said. Although his voice was low and didn't carry well, I was close enough to hear "Of course, since I don't know you, I wrote to the Bishop in your district to ask about you."

Each beat of my heart pumped slower and heavier than the one previous. My stomach somersaulted. I hadn't known about this letter.

"He said that outside of the normal curiosities that young folks have, that you're a good young man." Dat paused and I prayed silently that Freeman wouldn't crack a joke. "I'll be sad to see her move, but I know you'll take care of her."

"Yes, I will." Freeman stated emphatically. I was struck by the seriousness in his voice and the way he met Dat's eyes when he responded.

"You understand why we needed you to postpone the wedding, don't you?" Dat said after a short break in the conversation.

After a few beats Freeman replied. "March will work out just fine."

Then they moved onto a less stressful topic and I finally let the breath out that I'd been holding unknowingly.

The following day Freeman and I went by train to Ohio, and it was the longest stretch of time we'd ever had together. I pretended we were married and he treated me just as protectively as a husband would. He told me about his family and told me what to expect.

He'd met my quiet family and I could hardly imagine his, because according to his description they were the complete opposite.

During my days in Ohio I learned first-hand that his family really was quite different than mine. His dad John intimidated me some but his mom, Annie, made up for it with her smile that was as bright as her red hair. I learned that she was adopted into an Amish family. I had never heard of such a thing and was fascinated.

The family was free-spirited and proud. Nothing happened quietly, and they were constantly bantering with each other. They laughed loud and argued louder. What a change from my sober strict and traditional family. I'd always been taught to follow the letter of the law and do so quietly and with humility. I assumed all Amish communities were the same. Once we married and I moved to Ohio, I would really be on an adventure, and it excited me to my core. Even with all the differences, I felt at home there instantly.

The first evening I sat and watched everyone interact with each other. Everyone talked at once and answered each other at once. I didn't know how any of them kept up, but no one missed a beat. I also watched with curiosity as his mom made dinner. She had ground beef and began adding cracker crumbs, mashed potatoes, and all sorts of random garden vegetables.

Sel guckt vee schlop. I thought. That looks like slop.

Little did I know that the *slop* was delicious meatloaf. The perfect first meal with the family I would marry into. It was something completely new to me, filled with *everything*, and baked to perfection. I ate till I was full. For the first time in a long time my stomach was full as was my heart. This new family filled me with an excitement and a belonging that I'd always longed for. I was happy.

"I really love it out here, Freeman," I told him on a snowy blowy evening out. "Your family is so much fun and energetic."

We'd gone out visiting that evening, and there was a little snow on the road as Freeman drove the buggy back to his house. The snow was becoming heavier and heavier by the minute.

"Good ole Bill here is getting a little ornery," he commented about his horse. A grin crossed his face as the buggy began to go faster and faster.

Suddenly, the buggy wasn't just speeding, it was swerving crossways all over the road. Good ole Bill was scaring the daylights out of me.

"Yeehaw!" Freeman bellowed with a long line of laughter as he held the reigns tightly, but he didn't seem to be making a great effort to calm the skittish brute of a horse.

I didn't dare move a muscle for fear of being thrown from the buggy. I looked from Bill to Freeman, back and forth. Both were as spontaneous as the other, and I wasn't sure which one I felt like scolding. After several of the longest minutes of my life, Freeman gained control of the horse and slowed him down. Poor Bill was huffing and puffing for a while and let out a few good neighs in protest of his restriction, but I thought it served him right.

Freeman, on the other hand, seemed proud and exhilarated. I decided not to say anything to him about how frightened I was.

"Wasn't that fun?" he said, looking over at me. Then he started laughing, throwing his head back. "You can't fool me, Liddy, you're as white as a sheet."

"Freeman!" I gave him a playful slap on the arm, then chuckled a bit myself.

After Thanksgiving, a hired driver took us back to Dover but Freeman couldn't stay; he had to return to Ohio rather quickly. A week later I received a letter with the special words I had longed to hear.

I love you.

After that, the words came freely in every letter, carrying me through the winter months when it seemed spring would never come. We didn't see one another again until late March on the very cusp of spring, only a few days before our wedding.

Our wedding.

Our wedding.

Twenty

Living in Branford, Delaware (March 27–29, 1947)

When Summer Finally Arrives

I AWOKE TO a chill in the air that brought goose bumps to my arms. I rubbed them away and nestled beneath my old threadbare quilt a moment longer. The orange sunrise glanced through the unhemmed royal blue curtains, shining bright in my eyes. The delicate warmth bathed my face and I looked around noting my sisters were still asleep.

I swung my feet out from the covers and instinctively Bertha wrapped the additional yardage of blanket closer to her. The four walls of the room suddenly seemed small. Not just small for four girls, but too small for me. While this was not the room where I'd slept all my growing up years, it somehow represented all the rooms through the years of my youth. Four walls protecting me from the elements of the world, though it could do nothing to protect me from the burdens within—hunger, sickness, death. I purposed myself in the quiet moments of the morning never to lose sight of where I'd come from. To remember all that I'd learned in the spring of my life.

After freshening up, I began dressing for the day. I put on my typical black stockings, making sure there were no runs in them, and then laid my dark royal blue dress onto the bed. While the dress was new, I wasn't fond of the fabric. Still, I put it on meticulously, making sure every straight pin was in place. Over it, I put on my white organza cape and apron. Even though the clothing was far from new, it all looked crisp and ironed to perfection. I'd made sure of that. Next, I removed my sleeping bonnet and, with the use of the small handheld mirror I'd had most of my life, took my hair down, smoothed it out with a wet comb and put it back up. After inspecting my stray curls, I put on my black Sunday covering.

I went to my closet and took out my black Sunday shoes. Another thing I didn't particularly like, they seemed a little too mature for my twenty years, but they were shoes. I'd gone without shoes off and on throughout much of my life, so I wasn't about to complain now over a pair I didn't find beautiful. I laced them up my ankles, paying close attention to the hooks and eyes so as not to get them crisscrossed incorrectly.

I smoothed down my apron and let out a long breath—nervous about how I looked, and full of anticipation of what was to come. I looked again into the small mirror and inspected my eyes. Did they look tired? I knew of all days, I couldn't be tired today.

My wedding day.

I walked down the stairs, hearing Lavina in the kitchen preparing breakfast. I wore an extra apron so I wouldn't dirty my wedding garments and began helping her.

"Your sisters up?" She asked.

"They were just getting up," I told her. "They'll be down in a few minutes."

I looked around and admired the many cakes. Freeman and I had been up until four o'clock in the morning baking the cakes then washing all the dishes. What started out as something fun for us to do together ended with complete exhaustion. We fell asleep sitting upright in the chairs a few times before the job was done.

I peeked at the large wedding cake I'd baked and decorated myself earlier in the week. I was pleased with it. When I got to the punch bowl that would hold the variety of fruits and berries I felt a tug in my heart. I would have no grapes to drape around the outside of the bowl. Practically every reception had beautiful grapes draped in the fruit bowl. But, after looking everywhere, I couldn't find any. While I knew it was just grapes, it was important to me. Then, I knew I needed to stop daydreaming and help get a light breakfast on the table. Hungry men, including Freeman, would be in from the barn shortly.

When I spotted Freeman coming inside, I smiled at how his face had grown red from the cold. He looked so handsome even without wearing his wedding suit. He winked at me and went into the bedroom he'd shared with my brothers to get ready for our wedding.

By a quarter after seven my whole family had eaten and dressed for the two-mile buggy ride over to my mother's cousin, John Yoder's, home where the ceremony would be held. We had coupled up four of our friends who would be our attendants. One couple would drive us to the ceremony and sign our marriage license at the close of the day. Ira Nissley and my cousin Annie Swarzentruber, as two of our wedding attendants, *nava huckas*, drove Dat and Lavina in front of us, we were in the middle, and my family was behind us in several buggies.

Freeman helped me up, and once we got settled in the buggy with a blanket over our laps, I began feeling a little less anxious because Freeman was now with me. We wouldn't be separated for the remainder of the day. And now, almost alone, I finally had the chance to consider how handsome he looked in his navy suit. I liked the different collar that he wore beneath the suit coat; it laid down flat unlike the short collars that poked straight up like they wore in Dover. I was learning that Ohio did things differently, and it thrilled me.

As we headed out of the drive I saw the snow begin to fall. Tiny flakes blew everywhere around the buggy. It was beautiful.

"You know what they say about snow on your wedding day?" my sister Tillie said. She was also one of my attendants.

"We're going to be rich," Freeman piped up with his usual enthusiasm.

"I wouldn't get too excited," John Detwiler, another attendant, said from the driver's seat. "There's only a little snow."

"Well, maybe that means we'll just be a little bit rich," I said, leaning into Freeman.

When we arrived, things became almost a blur. While the routine of the service was not much different from an ordinary Sunday morning, time seemed to go quicker than I had anticipated.

At eight o'clock everyone was seated. Freeman and I occupied the front bench, facing the preacher. We all sang several songs—none that I had particularly picked out as special, but our typical long and slow songs, giving me plenty of time to get nervous again. I was pleased with the man chosen to lead the singing. His voice was rich and bold. During the songs, I couldn't help but consider my mom. Oh, how I longed for her to be there with me on this special day.

"In the garden," the Bishop said as he brought his message to a close, "Adam looked and looked for a mate but there was none to be found. He saw that the animals were not alone, but each having another to be a companion. Then God said that it wasn't good for Adam to be alone and Eve was created." He cleared his throat rather abruptly and then his voice went up a notch as he continued. "She was created to be his helper and to be at his side as the weaker of the two. That was the first marriage. But, oh, their sin and the sins of the generations to come then brought on the great flood. Oh, how disobedience can bring such destruction."

He went on to talk about the marriage relationships of Isaac and Rebecca and Jacob and Rachel and Leah, emphasizing the fact that God did not want them to mingle with the other nations. He spoke of Solomon and all of his wives, and how his sin brought the people into captivity.

"We must stay away from the world and look to Jesus as our holy example. Because we have the Bible, we can see the destruction that comes from disobedience. You start your marriage out here, in the sight of God. It is your duty to keep this commitment as a contract made between you and God."

He read I Corinthians 7 and Ephesians 5:2, and after making a few more remarks he looked at Freeman and me and said, "After you have thus learned and heard this ceremony you may come forward in the awesomeness of God."

Freeman and I stood and moved to stand in front of the Bishop. We kept our eyes down to show our humility, but how I wanted to look into Freeman's eyes and see them twinkle.

The Bishop went on to remind us of our duties as a married couple and asked us both in turn to affirm our commitment. Then he took Freeman's left hand and joined it with my left hand and, together with his, held them as he spoke a prayer over our union. Once he said, "Amen," he declared that we were now husband and wife and asked us to return to our seats. As we'd seen in all the other marriage ceremonies we'd attended, we kept our eyes downcast and made no move to attract any unusual attention.

The service was over and Freeman and I were instructed to go immediately to the buggy that was waiting to take us to Adam Byler's home for the reception. We were driven over to the house, and even in front of friends I was too shy to consider what had just taken place. I was a married woman. Freeman took my hand and squeezed it as if telling me I love you. I squeezed back.

Once arriving at the house, Freeman and I were shown to one of the bedrooms where we could put down our things. These were our first moments alone as husband and wife but I didn't close the bedroom door, as truly the only purpose was to exchange out my black covering for a white one. I was now married and would no longer need to wear a black covering for church services and events.

Freeman interrupted my busyness and took me gently into his arms. Though he had done this before I found there was a purpose in his touch that made me catch my breath. His eyes found mine just before he placed a perfect kiss on my lips, lingering for several wonderful moments. An adrenaline rush would not come close in explaining my reaction to his closeness. My life was about to change. My heart was secured. I was treasured in a way that I didn't realize was possible.

After reluctantly releasing my hold on him, I checked myself in the small mirror and secretly wondered if I looked different. Did I look older and more like a wife? Then for a moment I pictured Memm smiling back, giving me permission now to move on with the next stage of my life that would be far away from everything I knew. I smiled at my reflection and went on to the reception with my husband. I not only felt ready for the rest of the day of activity, but I was ready to be my husband's wife and to follow my mom's footsteps, the greatest wife and mother I knew. It brought a swelling to my heart to consider that Freeman was mine—all mine.

Before Freeman and I found our way to our corner table, my grandpa, Gideon Byler, found me. He bounced up to us even lighter than normal with a wide smile on his face. I loved my *daudy*, my grandpa, for his cheerfulness. How I would miss him. He was the first to truly come to us and greet us at the reception.

"Liddy, do you see anything different at your corner table?" he asked, practically beaming.

I peered over to the corner table, noting that the royal blue curtains were pulled back nicely, letting the sun show through the window. The fruit bowl sat right there in the midst, our plates waiting for the hearty meal to come shortly. A kerosene lamp sat in the center as well.

"I don't," I said, knowing that he was so eager for me to notice *something.* "Maybe I should get closer."

"Look at your fruit bowl."

I gasped. "Grapes." While there were only very few small clusters, I had my grapes after all. "But how?"

"I searched in every town around here, determined that you should have your grapes. I barely made it to your ceremony on time." He set his jaw. "There were only a few when I found them, but now you have grapes to drape around your punch bowl. And, you make sure to enjoy them, okay?"

I hugged my *daudy*, thanking him. What a sweet soul he had been to do this for me. When he walked away, happy and pleased with himself, his steps were as light as a child's.

Freeman and I walked the rest of the way to our corner table and I admired the grapes once more. The house was filling up with people, and once the silent prayer was observed, the table waiters began their work. After so many years of nearly starving, I ate and ate. Freeman also devoured the meal and especially enjoyed several helpings of pie. After we slaved over them together for the entire previous night, they made a delicious reward for our hard work.

As evening approached my white cake was brought out to me. Even though it was only white I had used sliced English walnuts around the edges and corners for decoration. Freeman and I cut the cake and first served all of our cooks, table waiters, and attendants. After that the main cake and the variety of others Freeman and I baked were free to be eaten by anyone. We opened gifts and talked with friends and family. I savored my time with the people I'd known my whole life, not sure when I'd see them again.

And Freeman, *my husband*, also seemed to be enjoying himself. Because of the weather, only his parents were able to come for the wedding. I was sure he wished that his siblings and grandparents could've been there, but he seemed to not let it affect his happy-go-lucky personality. We chuckled and bantered with each other, but the day was mostly filled with activity and talking to our guests.

As the older married couples said their good-byes, the young people sat at the long benches and began their Singing. Their voices sounded beautiful, and Freeman and I happily joined in. After a time of singing and prayer, the young people went outside to commence with their typical Singing activities. I didn't mind skipping these merry games; I was a married woman now. I wouldn't be mingling or attending Singings any longer. The nostalgia of the years behind me and all the worry of ever finding the right man warmed me. I touched Freeman's arm in response, and while I didn't say a word, our eyes met, and I was sure he knew what I was thinking.

The next morning seemed almost overly common, except that we awoke at Adam Byler's home. After getting dressed, I went to help with breakfast, and Freeman went outside to help with the chores. There was little conversation, only the knowing. The knowing that we were married.

After breakfast dishes were cleared and cleaned, Freeman and I loaded up the buggy for a day full of returning the dishes used for the reception. We drove all over our rural community and enjoyed the light-hearted conversation we could share without worry of being alone too long as an unmarried couple. Never again would we have a bus schedule telling us what time we would have to say good-bye.

I had noted for several days that Dat was growing older. His smile was not as ready and his shoulders seemed to hang just a little too much. It reminded me of the weeks and months that followed Memm's death. This time he wasn't grieving death, he was grieving my departure. My heart ached.

This would be the morning I would travel to my new home with my husband and my in-laws. I would be given a fresh start in a new town, with a new community, a new house—everything would be new. But, oh, how bitter it felt to say good-bye to my family. I knew that life would go on as normal in Delaware. By that evening my responsibilities would be split up among my sisters. Maybe my absence would not make such a huge dent in my large family. But I would miss them and the quiet connection I shared with Dat and my sisters and brothers.

We all ate breakfast together, just as always. I was up early enough to help, of course. We worked in the kitchen as we always did and ate together as a family as usual, with the addition of Freeman and his parents. While some would love to have the fanfare of their new marriage be acknowledged at every turn, for me, it felt so comfortable to do the daily tasks with Freeman near me, knowing that when he went home, I would go too.

I knelt in my bedroom, after breakfast, filling my small trunk with the few things I truly owned. I patted the top of everything down and laid my black shawl on top. It was the last gift Memm had given me on my sixteenth birthday, less than a month before her death. I took a moment to consider it and touched it as if it were the most delicate silk, though it was wearing thin. I pulled it out and decided to travel with it. Surely any extra warmth would be appreciated on this chilly day. Freeman came in, latched the trunk, and carried it outside. I left the room and closed the door, telling myself it was time to move on. I walked slowly down the hall, knowing what was coming. My family stood in the living room, waiting to say good-bye, each trying to look happy for me.

Little Betty cried and cried when I hugged her. I couldn't keep from crying myself. She was so young when Memm died; I had been a mother to her for the last four years. I gave each of my siblings a hug, but when I came to Dat I stood in front of him, heartbroken. Both his hands wrapped around my small hands, consuming them. He didn't cry but his eyes were burdened with sadness.

"I hope your life gives you all that you dream," he said in his low, resonate voice that always felt like a warm blanket around me, familiar and comforting.

While the feeling was vastly different, Dat and I had grown accustomed to leaning on each other after Memm died. Of course, he had a wife now, but our relationship was just as strong, our memories of our life with Memm just as ready in our minds. Those days where nothing was simple, yet they were the most precious of times. The meager meals around the rickety table, the beautiful moments when our family was introduced to the newest baby, the joy of reading and singing together. Even a weak cup of Postum would find a soft spot in my heart forevermore. How I would miss my dad.

As we left my little farmhouse I waved until I was sure they couldn't see me anymore. I pictured Memm waving back at me from the kitchen window, where she had often waved to departing company. I settled back down, cozily nestled next to my husband, and looked around knowing that the buds on the trees were only weeks away from showing themselves. We were on the very cusp of spring. But for me, spring was complete.

Summer had just begun.

The Author

Elizabeth Byler Younts is the granddaughter of Lydia Lee Coblentz. She is a member of the American Christian Fiction Writers. She is an Air Force Officer's wife with two young daughters, making a home wherever they are currently stationed. Please visit her at www.elizabethbyleryounts.com.

About Liddy

 Lydia Lee Coblentz resides in Vermontville, MI. She is often found sitting in her hickory rocker entertaining guests with her stories and feisty spirit. She especially enjoys expected and unexpected company and large family reunions. Lydia currently has eight living children (one son has passed), forty-four grandchildren, over seventy great grandchildren with several more on the way, including her first great great grandchild. Her birthday is October 26, 1926; she loves birthday cards and handwritten letters. Please visit www.elizabethbyleryounts.com for correspondence information.

Made in the USA
Lexington, KY
14 September 2012